The Hand Behind The Word

Handwriting Analysis
JAQS* Style

The Hand Behind The Word

Handwriting Analysis
JAQS* Style

JERRAL SAPIENZA

LLX Press
Eugene, Oregon

BY JERRAL SAPIENZA

LLX PRESS
LIFELONG LEARNING EXCELLENCE, INC.
Post Office Box 380
Eugene, OR 97440-0380 =USA=

PROJECT DESIGN : JAY SCOT
COVER DESIGN: ANDY KERR, AKERRDESIGN, LLC

First Edition   January 2005
First Printing
R93d

ISBN: 0-9717107-3-2
Library of Congress Control Number: 2004092162

Available separately for collection of samples:
*JAQS Handwriting Samples
Collections Booklet*
ISBN: 0-9717107-6-7

For online information about handwriting analysis, visit:
WWW.HWA.ORG

Handwriting's Palace

Façades and flags, arches and windows,
Dark hidden hallways, doorways and gates,
Moat with its sentries, turrets and cannon,
Drawbridge and chains hold back certain traits.

The goings and the comings of the business of the day.
Closets of deceit and tales of yesterday;
Hopes for future's callings and fears of what might be,
Skills and talents known and not, traits of artistry.

Also by Jerral Sapienza:

Urgent Whispers: Care of the Dying
A Personal Reference Manual for Friends and Family
Assisting a Loved One at the End of Life

JAQS Handwriting Samples Collection Book
A Companion Samples Collection

ACKNOWLEDGEMENTS

This book had been one of my back-burner projects for years. Finally in April 2001, it started cooking, thanks to then high school student Marley Adkins whose senior project on Handwriting Analysis required a mentor. Notes for our seven months of weekly classes became the skeleton for *The Hand Behind The Word*.

Special thanks to Chris Ransdell, Mollie McMillan, Kristyan Clouse, Autumn Wise, Sean Podvent, Roseann Raymond, John Freshwater and Mama Mecu each for their faith, support and contribution in their special way. Thanks to Lynn Olsen, Carol Harrison, Dennis Boehm, Robert Jones and Kacie O'Shannon for eagle eye edit and proofs and Kerry Marshall of Brighton, England for first international review.

Thanks also to Andy Kerr for his many contributions toward a finer project. His cover design surpassed all expectations and continues to entertain folks. Andy also made the case for swapping the title and subtitle to what it is now. Kudos also to Michael McMillan for his many entertaining handwriting samples over the years, one of which caught Andy's eye for the back cover and sample book.

I am indebted to my parents, John and Fern Sapienza, for their support and non-judgment over the years of my curious fascination with handwriting. And to my son Adam, always close to my heart, thanks for being you. Adam's first sample from years ago, age three, is the cute little sideways man on the cover.

And, of course, thanks to the thousands of writers who have written in my sample books over the years and to the historical writers whose signatures have found their way into this collection from various corners of time and geography.

One of the most delightful gifts of handwriting for which I am ever thankful is its ability to allow all of us to commune again with friends and family who have passed on since writing in a sample book. Though they are gone, they are still very much alive there, beaming from the pages of a sample. I love being able to visit with them again by just turning a page.

Finally, Thank You, Readers, for your curiosity and interest in the subject of handwriting analysis. I hope it brings you as much enjoyment and fascination in the coming years as it has brought me all my life. Have a delightful time!

Eugene, Oct, 2004

Table of Contents

1

Handwriting The Stuff
Inky Squiggles on a Page

2

Mechanics of Handwriting
How it All Works

3

Beginnings
Starting Out as Handwriting Analyst

4

Saints and Criminals
Some Special Views of Handwriting

5

Cultural And Historical Perspectives
in Handwriting

6

The JAQS Sample Format

The Digits in Handwriting, Too

7

Changing Your Handwriting
Changing your life

8

From the Other Side of the Table:
Values, Mindset and Ethics

9

Personal Relations & Compatibility Studies
Browsing Handwriting for Learning

10

Handwriting Analysis for People Managers
Using Handwriting in the Workplace

11

Putting It All Together
Taking Your First Handwriting Samples

12

Archetypes and Elements
Systems for Better Organization

13

Trait Compendium and Glossary of
Handwriting Traits and Their Meaning

A Closing Word

Appendix I
Creating a JAQS Sample Book

Appendix II
JAQS Sample Archiving

Index

" Colui che apprenderà che gli è possibile riconoscere i pensieri, l'indole e la disposizione dello scrittore, per mezzo di una lettera intima, ridarà o si meraviglierà grandemente. "

– *Prof Camillo Baldo, Bologna 1622*
Grandfather of Modern Handwriting Analysis

Introduction

Handwriting analysis is an intriguing blend of story teller, psychologist, detective and personal advisor magically materializing out of a page of handwriting to show and tell us amazing things about life. Handwriting has fascinated me since I was seven years old and first saw those lines and loops, tics and swoops laying on a page. The shapes and spaces, form and feel of this encoded person-to-person communication have always spoken to me far beyond the content of any message.

Until I was a junior in High School, I thought that everyone saw in handwriting what I saw. But that year in a writing class when I was working on a debate project with a group of classmates, I learned this wasn't true. We were trying to decide who would be our lead debater. I glanced at a page of writing left by one of our members who was not present that day and, pointing to the page, said I knew Eric would be great at debate and would probably be a good lead.

Puzzled, the group looked at me, then at the page, and asked if Eric had told me anything about these skills of his. "No," I said, "but look at the way he makes a 7." I pointed to some digits on the handwritten page before us. My classmates only stared at me, then at the paper, then back at me. Clearly they were not seeing what I saw.

I learned that day that not only did they not see anything in that 7, but they also thought it rather freakish that I insisted there was anything there to see. No matter how clearly I pointed out to them the shape of the 7 and tried to explain what it meant of his ability to hold firm to his point, they were completely unconvinced of our friend's ability to argue or of my own ability to contribute anything useful to this discussion.

Given the rather quiet, bookish lad that I was at the time, (and perhaps given the fact that my 7 didn't at the time have the argumentative tic in the upper left that it has today), I quietly conceded. I decided that perhaps they were right and there was nothing to it. I would keep my mouth shut until I knew more.

But I never stopped observing handwriting, collecting samples and working on a compendium of traits and patterns I noticed over the years. I just learned not to talk much about it. Until, that is, I was able to have a much stronger case to present and an audience who wanted to listen. Out of those many quiet years of research and collection came the *JAQS Style* handwriting sample format on which this book is based.

Times have changed in those many years since high school. Nowadays I talk of handwriting in boardrooms and fellowship halls, dating services and law offices, government agencies, grange halls, conference auditoriums, dinner parties, business meetings, on radio and television.

People really do care about the stories handwriting reveals of themselves and the people around them. They want to learn more and they want it codified in a teachable, definable way so that they can apply it themselves to their lives, their work and their learning style.

I believe that the current volume will serve to do just that: help teach in a way that any reader can apply in daily life. One thing you are encouraged to do is get involved. Go out and collect some of your own samples to add to those you see here.

You will find in the book over a hundred samples from my personal archives, drawn from the last twenty years of research and collection in all walks of life, in several different countries. I have included some samples from other cultures and languages as well to help demonstrate the value of cross-cultural applicability of some of these principles of handwriting analysis.

Especially in the case of the personal samples for the section on Saints and Criminals, Chapter Four, I have attempted to use as many older samples as possible. This is because there are some harsh traits here which the writers may prefer to forget. I believe it is a good idea to give writers the benefit of the doubt and assume that in the passing years they've grown immeasurably, well beyond any negative traits and traumas I show in their hands here.

Although I have had no contact with most of these writers for years, I like to envision every writer as having grown and prospered in the years since, living a healthy life, having a wholly functional hand were we to sample it anew today.

With the exception of historical figures and my own, no samples in the book contain names, signatures or any identifying information. I have recast some details of lives in order to protect privacy. Every writer in the book consented to offering a *JAQS Sample* and participated freely in the research project. They were also all given feedback at the time on their handwriting.

Sampled writers, if they see the book, will recognize their hand and my comments about it from when we spoke. Some, especially those from Chapter Four, may find that what I said in person was much more congenial and less harsh than some of what I say here.

Not that my readings have a reputation for being fluff. Quite the contrary. One of my colleagues used to chide me for being as she said, *too direct* with writers. "Jerral," she would say with a smile when we were on break between samples. "Don't you have anything *positive* to say about anyone's handwriting?"

She exaggerates a bit. I do try to keep a reading as balanced as possible. But she is right: when I err, it is typically on the side of being too direct with a writer and definitely not too soft and fluffy.

Nonetheless, there are some harsher aspects of a hand I am not likely to bring up with a writer in person, if we only have a few minutes to discuss things. As you will see in Chapter Eight, on Ethics and Etiquette for Handwriting Analysts, there are some ethical considerations as to how and what we say and when. Here in the book where anonymity is assured and many years have passed, some of the direct negative points become useful teaching points.

One note on the size and clarity of samples presented here: the *JAQS Style* sample format is almost as large as a page of text in this book. In most cases it would be impractical to include them at full size. So in the interest of giving you access to more samples and make as many points as clearly as possible, most of the samples you will see here are either reduced in size and resolution, or cropped to include only a portion of the sample.

Many samples were also on colored paper with writing bleeding through from the other side. We tried to clean them up as much as possible. But the value of a particular trait for teaching outweighed the perfection of a graphic image in these selections, so some choices are smudged. Perhaps a workbook with just samples at full size and resolution is in order. Meanwhile, you'll see many smaller and rough hewn samples among hundreds presented here.

I welcome you on this adventure into handwriting! I also encourage you to make best use of it by collecting some samples of your own from your world, your people, your family whom you know so well. As you look at the materials presented here in a context of your own sample base, it becomes a much more rich and valuable resource for you to ponder and draw upon.

I continue to collect and study handwriting everywhere I go, every opportunity I get. I have collected literally thousands of samples, one person at a time, everywhere I've been. Whenever I see handwriting, it is not the message that draws me into yet another sample, but that fascinating essence of the *hand behind the word*.

1

Handwriting The Stuff
Inky Squiggles on a Page

The *hand behind the word* is not really a radical idea. But it is one which people tell me they never thought about until they started to study handwriting. They have looked at, or at least seen, handwriting all their lives. Yet they haven't been looking with any thought as to what else might be in the message other than "just inky squiggles on a page."

Depending on which handwriting you look at, you may see it as a pleasant note or a messy scrawl you wish were easier to read. But you may not have given much thought before to the essence and spirit of the writer, the ghost in the letters, the story of the placement reflecting the writer who put it that way. But once you do, it seems it's almost impossible not to see it in all handwriting everywhere.

We use the term *hand* to mean both the handwriting as an object and the essence of the writer's expression represented by the handwritten form. Strokes and traits together embodied in the hand will represent both the personality of the writer who wrote it, as well as a kind of cultural signature from which the writer came.

Handwriting as Reflection of Life

Handwriting in some form has probably been around since the first caveman storyteller needed to make a note to remind himself of which parts of the tale he forgot. But even today, all these eons and lifetimes later, the concept of handwriting hasn't changed a lot. Sure, we have other fancy electronic devices now to keep us from using it much, but when we write by hand it's still the same basic idea as it was thousands of years ago: represent the concepts and reminders of what it is we want to hold onto by converting them to an alphabetic form and scratching them across a flattish surface with a sharp stick.

The politics of handwriting has gotten a little more complex over the last few thousand years. The world is split into more than a few factions as to which characters to include as alphabet, which side of the page writing starts on and what direction it flows. But all in all its function hasn't changed much in all these thousands of years.

Handwriting is first a social system's communication tool. People put into it whatever energy and expression is in them at the time. Just as they might do in a conversation with you, when they get really excited they lean into it with a forward intentional motion, pushing their ideas ahead of them in a flowing directional way. They move across and down a page, applying a sense of rules, relationship and boundaries as they go. Their sense of personal preference, style and experience flow into the writing just as when they move, gesture, speak or act out their needs.

Elements of Handwriting

One of the most interesting things about handwriting is how basic it is at its core. We make our point or record our message by our choice of placement of a series of patterned marks on a page.

Although it may seem odd to break it down so simply, all alphabets of all handwriting are essentially only a series of three strokes:

- A vertical line, |
- A horizontal line, —
- A circle. O

Everything else is a variation of repetitions or combinations of these three thematic strokes in a pattern and structure of how and where we choose to place them. So we make our swoops and flurries, our angles and signature essentially out of variations of these three single strokes. As we string strokes together in our own unique way out comes a message in more than just words.

With the message comes a picture half-drawn, half-stenciled; half-word, half-whisper using the language of the alphabet as patterns on a page leaving a secondary message layer as well.

Handwriting's First Job

The first layer of any message is the words made up of an alphabet we subscribed to over the course of our many years of writing. Whether we know it or not, whether we like it or not, how well we fit or fail to fit into the accepted variations of this cultural alphabet affects our ability to communicate. In order to work most effectively, handwriting's first job is to communicate. It does not necessarily have to conform to the copy-book structure we learned in school as basic fourth-grade penmanship. But it has to work.

If we write upside down and backwards like Leonardo da Vinci's secret writing to himself, or if we make arbitrary changes for new letters of the alphabet, we do not enhance our handwriting's first job. Handwriting needs first to be understood in order to be useful.

Acceptable forms of handwriting will vary from culture to culture and even generation to generation. What passes for acceptable in schools today would not likely have been tolerated even as recently as twenty or thirty years go. But our reliance on computers and other non-handwritten forms of communication has had some dramatic effects on society. It is no surprise that it affects handwriting as well.

With the advent of computers, daily handwriting in our culture has been on the decline. It is still used, of course and that's why we can still study it. But it's far less prevalent these days than before the 1980's when computers began to emerge. In the 1990's there was an absolute boom in their use due to transference of a huge portion of daily communication to email and the Internet. We're not far enough away from those days just yet to see what effects the digitalization of communication will have on handwriting studies in the future, but there will almost certainly be even more repercussions.

Natural Variations in Handwriting

Every writer will have natural fluctuations affecting handwriting over time for a variety of different reasons. Among the more basic ones:

- Sleepiness, Agitation, Anger or Emotions
- Injury to the hand
- Variations in available light and vision
- Illness, especially neurological illnesses
- Writing with the non-dominant hand
- Position of the writing space and page
- Difference in type of pen
- Method of holding the pen
- Training and aptitude in art, architecture, etc.
- Fine motor coordination / manual dexterity
- Age and educational experience
- Profession and amount of daily writing

Different professions use handwriting different amounts of time, so we can't judge everyone on the same basis. For instance, someone who has worked as a woodsman for the last twenty years is apt to have very different handwriting than someone who has worked as a writer or teacher or librarian for twenty years. Not that all woodsmen or all librarians will write alike, but when people work in professions where they read and write handwritten notes on a daily basis, they are apt to have very different handwriting from someone who only uses it occasionally.

We also need to bear in mind that even one writer's handwriting will vary quite significantly over time, with some of these variations in play. Think about your own writing and how and when it fluctuates or how it differs from what it was years ago. When you look at other people's handwriting it's good to think about these things and realize that there may be other reasons, too, to explain some of the variations you may see.

Whispers and Shadows in the Hand

In addition to all of the environmental and social variables, there are many personal design and personal taste factors which will contribute to the variation in writing. Among them:
- how much pressure we use
- our personal sense of artistry or simplicity
- our structure and form
- slant, size and slope
- how we shape and link each character
- line density and thickness
- where we choose to place characters on the page
- ligatures and links of particular letter combinations

All of these and others are consciously or unconsciously, intentionally or unintentionally, choices we make in the first few seconds as we begin to write any message.

Once a message is made of alphabet and form to satisfy its first job of communicating the basic point, handwriting has much more to express. It also forms a transcript and history of the filters and passages of the writer's life. It mimics our values, beliefs, fears, life experience, relationships, emotions and even our health. Quietly encoded there in the lines and loops and tics and swoops of a handwritten message is a secondary whisper, a fascinating second message waiting to be opened by anyone who realizes it is there.

Conscious or unconscious, intentional or unintentional, there will always be more than just the text of any handwritten message. It is the handwriting analyst's task and treasure to spend a little time with these emergent whispers of the message and reflect back to the writer some of the gifts and challenges shown there, from a little deeper in those expressive shadows.

An Invitation To Learn, Grow and Share

The Hand Behind the Word doesn't claim to be a book to teach you all there is to know about handwriting. But it will give you some of the keys to the kingdom and welcome you back to these pages as you begin to apply what you learn. Different from other books you may have seen, its perspective on handwriting is to relate your studies to many other aspects of life, from body mechanics to ethics, business, psychology, personal growth, relationship, history and even a bit about deception, prayer, elemental archetypes and astrology.

You are encouraged to learn, grow and share your journey with others, collecting handwriting from friends and family and sharing with them some of what you learn as you look into their samples. You will learn best what you seek to apply and practice. If you come upon a term or reference in the book which is unclear or confusing to you, Chapter Thirteen's Trait Compendium and Glossary may help clarify it.

Learning about handwriting doesn't require your full time attention. In fact, it's best if you can begin by incorporating it into whatever you already do. Whether you are a beginner or a professional, a student, business leader, peace officer, politician, office worker, homemaker, educator, or even a retired minister: whatever your interests, you are invited to grow a little. Sit back and enjoy yourself as you meet new ideas and new people in your handwriting studies.

If I've done my job right, whatever your opinions about handwriting coming into the book, your view is about to change. You can expect some topics here to fascinate you, some to possibly offend you; some to agree with what you've always thought, some to challenge your beliefs; some to encourage your handwriting just as it is and some to encourage you to change it. I want to get you involved with your handwriting. I want you to learn, grow and share along this journey.

Every journey of a lifetime begins with a single step: eager, curious, questioning and bold. You are invited on this journey of foundation and fascination, a study in handwriting to take a new first step toward better understanding yourself and others through the mysteries decoded from the *hand behind the word.*

2

Mechanics of Handwriting
How it All Works

The differences in handwriting between males and females is more than just an illusion. Although there will always be exceptions, appearances tend to suggest that men's handwriting is often less developed and calls upon a narrower range of motion with predictable middling effects. Women's handwriting often seems more creative and unique with a better infusion of their personality coming across in the hand. These differences are not just sexism propagated by men to excuse their unsightly scrawl. There are biological reasons why men and women's writing develops differently.

At the time when boys and girls are first beginning to write, their young bodies are developing at different rates. In our culture, at about age six or seven when we generally start to write cursive, children are still struggling to develop and tune their fine-motor skills. Boys at this age tend to have less fine-motor coordination than girls. As a result boys' handwriting is generally not as well defined or developed as the girls'.

In an effort to keep up, boys will often try to abandon cursive altogether and revert back to the manuscript or printing they learned a year or two earlier. They often regard the new fine-motor-required cursive as an overwhelming challenge to their success, so will try to shirk failure by competitively returning to their success at printing.

A good teacher at this age will take into account the differences in development between boys and girls and will gently but firmly insist that the boys keep improving their cursive. As long as it is expected that the boys succeed and they are not treated as defective or failures, then they will do as well at cursive as the girls. But boys who are allowed to get away with messy cursive or revert back to manuscript printing will just add to the ranks of men who claim as adults, "Oh, I just never write in cursive."

Unfortunately for these boys, their loss is one they may not recognize until many years later when they realize they lack aptitudes, skills or interest in art and fine-motor skills. The reason is very basic. Just at the time when their body was approaching readiness to acquire new skills about how to deal with the demands of fine-motor motion and creative detail, they went charging off in another direction and rambunctiously went back to being a rowdy little boy with rougher more noisy games to play.

This is not to say that there is only one stage of life where we can acquire our various skills. A commitment at any age to refine the handwriting can improve it. But as with music, athletics or skills acquiring multiple languages, there are often stages in life where the body and mind are more susceptible to effortless and easier learning.

Life's Telltale Signs in Handwriting

There are other life experiences besides lack of fine-motor development which show up in a child's handwriting. When there is a case of severe trauma or distress in a child, there are always telltale signs in the hand. Adults store their life story in their handwriting as well, but it begins as a child. Since children are newer to the learning system with less experience and inertia of habit to draw them back on track, life stresses will affect a child's handwriting in a much more pronounced way than a similar stress load will affect an adult's hand. Adults will be affected but the effect is temporary. For a child, the effect can be a lifelong aberration stored quietly in the handwriting.

Especially in cases of abandonment, abuse, family alcoholism, high psychological trauma, emotional distress, personality disorders and significant lack of self-esteem, a child's handwriting will often be severely altered. Depending on the learning stage where the trauma occurs, the handwriting may reflect a stunted formation. In severe cases, that stunted form persists well into adulthood and as a result many psycho-social problems from decades ago show up immediately in an adult's handwriting sample.

Be careful, however, about generalizations. Just because a child's handwriting is messy or lacking in readability, that does not always mean there is a major problem. It is important to consult a competent child psychologist before jumping to conclusions based solely on handwriting. Teens will almost always have significant fluctuations in their hand because of the major physical, emotional and ideological changes they undergo during this phase of life.

We cannot analyze children's handwriting by the same standards as adults. If we were to come across an adult's hand which looked like this fourteen year old boy's, flags might go up and bells might ring. We may label the writer as unstable and perhaps anti-social. But as a fourteen year old boy, it's just not that uncommon. Although teen boys can be delightful young men in process, most can also be quite angry, anti-social and lacking in self-esteem, all of which show up in this sample. Luckily, the large majority will outgrow this phase. They will grow up to be well-adjusted adults, contributing to lives of sanity and productivity.

If we were to see a young man in his mid-twenties or older with a sample like this one, then bells should ring loudly. At fourteen they would just jingle a bit. This is not to excuse messy handwriting at any age; it is never too early or too late to help someone improve. But a teenager has a lot on his plate, so we usually pick our battles more carefully. One of the best ways to help this boy improve his handwriting would probably be to support him in his life. Let's see who he is at twenty or twenty-five and then we'll talk.

A Teen Girl's Handwriting

Let's look at a young girl's handwriting from about the same age. Since teenage girls tend to self-police and judge one another for most everything, handwriting included, the great majority of girls at that age have very similar, very puffy, bubbly, quite neat looking handwriting like this, or similarly round but cursive:

Take a look at this next one. We immediately notice it is quite unusual because unlike boys, girls at fourteen generally have neater and more stable handwriting yet this one is neither. Her sense of placement and form is completely skewed and off. She doesn't know who or where she is. When I saw this girl's messy hand, I knew she was having some serious difficulties and it's likely more than just at school.

Her 3's 5's and 6's, though messy, are all fairly normal and well developed. We'll get more into the meanings of the individual digits later in Chapter Six, but just briefly: 3's show how we get along with friends and neighbor relations. Hers suggest that she gets along well with her peers and performs well at school where she feels comfortable and supported.

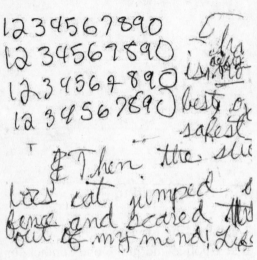

5's are our sense of humor and how we deal with organization and time issues. Her 5's say she has a well-adjusted (and probably ironic and dry) sense of humor, that she is intelligent and well organized.

6's are the way we deal with the minor irritation or minor traumas of life. In general, she's pretty effective there. But her 6's are a little slow and heavy which suggest that she's probably taking on a little more social burden than she needs to, such as not speaking up to defend herself.

The stab into the center of the 9 is disturbing, as are the 7's, 4's and 2's, not to mention all the scribbled disorderly writing around the edges. I would suspect that there is a divorce in process when this is happening. Those knives in the 9's are probably a direct reflection of what she's heard her mother and father tossing back and forth at each other. 9's have to do with sense of reputation and profession. This poor child is caught in the middle and her self esteem is suffering dramatically. She is blaming herself for it all.

Certainly at fourteen she has little reason to be concerned about her own job or professional reputation except as student. So the trouble in her 9's is almost certainly the reflection of a parent's sense of self-defeat. Same with the 4's. 4's have to do with intimate relationships and sexuality and at fourteen it is unlikely her 4 would be so unstable. That is also likely related to what she's hearing between her parents, although with all of the messy convoluted writing there is also a possibility of abuse.

The 7's, unfortunately, are more likely to be her own. And that's not good news. Since 7's reflect the sense of principles, hers at this point must seem completely confused and foundering. This is likely caused by emotional trauma which is affecting her ability to know what is right and wrong. This young woman has had to grow up way too fast and she must be undergoing some very difficult questioning traumas.

One reason that we'd let the boy off, by the way, without trying to delve too far into his life situation and mood swings is that most of his digits are fairly normal, or at least, the way they are abnormal is just in self-centered typical teenage boy ways. Not so with this girl's hand. Hers are much more affected in ways reflective of trauma. It's not just an angry angular lack of completing a particular stroke. She's got lots of extra strokes and pieces in the way she makes the digits.

This hand was a tough one to look at, especially when I saw her mother's. I could see then too much of the story and could just imagine the harshness and difficulties this young woman had to endure. I remember she seemed so foreign to her life. When she came in with her mother I noticed she was dressed like she was a time traveler coming out of another century, arriving here from the 1950's. In retrospect I decided it could be a symbolic message to think about how much society has changed in this last fifty years and how it has affected everything, including handwriting.

Social and Personal Influences in Handwriting

Our society has changed enormously in the last fifty years. One major symptom of its changes has been to gradually extend the age of adolescence into the twenties. Handwriting seems to have been affected by that, too, tending to settle into a stable form rather later than it did fifty years ago. At that time, the age at which a teen's handwriting tended to stabilize in form was between ages sixteen to eighteen for boys and fourteen to sixteen for girls. But these days it has shifted in conjunction with today's delayed onset of adulthood to somewhere in the neighborhood of age nineteen to twenty-two. That is a fairly significant shift.

Some will say that this is due to a decline in the educational system. Others will say it's a result of kids writing less and using computers more. Still others will say that it's a result of society's lack of formative rite of passage rituals for teens growing into adults and the feeling of confusion and alienation which results. Whatever the case, handwriting is definitely tending to stabilize later as evidenced by samples taken over the decades.

One possible explanation as to why children's handwriting is making that passage into adulthood later than it did before is that our society's priorities have shifted so much in the last fifty years. Since the 1950's the Baby Boomers have dramatically affected everything about society and its choices. Not surprisingly, their attitudes toward family and children have been very different from previous generations and that may well have even affected handwriting. Certainly it has affected the way their kids see life.

In Chapter Four we'll discuss a special handwriting trait like the one below found in the particular generation of kids I call the CoCos, the Children of the Children of the Sixties, that first generation of the Boomers' kids. As they were in their teens and twenties like the twenty-four year old here, they often had a common handwriting trait which, because of the excessive use of

CAPs, echoed some of the pain they may have felt as Children of the Children of the Sixties. Theirs was a very different generational hand than any we've seen before. It was louder and more defiant, more needing to be heard and listened to. Look at the confused and frustrated CAPs peppered all through this hand. They whisper of pain, loss of control and need to be noticed, even when the content of the message may seem silly like this one.

> I love Jerral he's such a Beautiful radiated being of lae & light a bit brutish sometimes but — that's exciting ya know!

It's a little late now to listen to these kids as children since many are in their thirties now and parents themselves. But it's still good advice. We need to pay attention to the children, answer their questions. Help them better understand this crazy world around them which is not of their making. More on the CoCos and their generational hand a bit later.

We should not be surprised that handwriting would be affected by societal changes. It is, after all, linked not only with the mechanics of the body but also with the emotional and intellectual experience present in the body of society as well.

What your handwriting looks like and how you choose to write didn't just happen. It evolved from the culturally developed writing patterns you were taught in school and from your body's mechanical and developmental ability to imitate these patterns through your fine-motor and hand-to-eye coordination. It's more than just mechanical or experiential, but that's part of it. The handwriting of the young girl above couldn't help but reflect her family situation, no matter how hard she tried to hide it.

Machines that Write

To think a moment about the process of cause and effect in writing, let's look at a couple of machines which do a kind of writing as well. Think, for instance, of a seismograph which is used in geology to measure movement of the earth during an earthquake. From sensors placed deep in the earth, a seismograph feels signals of the tremor and then writes a series of squiggly little lines scratched across a page to represent the intensity and duration of the earth tremors in action.

Or consider the electroencephalograph, EEG which is used in medicine to measure electrical signals across various points in the brain. From sensors placed on the scalp or in some cases implanted directly into the brain the EEG monitors tiny electrical changes in brain activity and then writes a series of squiggly little lines scratched across a page to represent the intensity and duration of these signals between brain nodes.

The Human Body as Writing Machine

The way machines write is similar to the way our body writes. The machines are dependent upon an event or motion which they then report very accurately by squiggling lines on a page accordingly. But a major difference between the machines and humans is that machines do a good job of filtering out background noise such that any two events of the same magnitude and duration will be reported predictably and identically by any number of like machines over any time period.

Like the seismograph and EEG which filter out as much background noise as possible in order to isolate the data signal, whenever we sit down to write, we *attempt* to filter out the background noise of our emotional state, our family problems, our caffeine tremors, or fear of a bad grade on that test we're writing.

But unlike the EEG or seismograph machines, our delicate body's writing machine is composed of approximately 78% water which is indeed very difficult to still. At the core of this watery system's nervous activity is our central nervous system, literally billions of nervous little cells, each ready to beam its active signal and communicate what it knows, what it feels, where it has been.

The EEG and seismograph both have fairly effective filtration systems for shielding against background noise. But this personal watery nervous system of ours has almost a zero percent chance of not being affected by the background noise of memories, feelings, history and environment it must pass through on the way to scratch out its message on the unsuspecting page. The noise always shows through. And that, for a handwriting analyst, is very good news.

As we write, our handwriting is very susceptible to our life experience, memories and feelings up to and including the moment when we sit down to write. While we write we tend to become involved in the processing of our words and thoughts. It's not just a matter of putting a few words on a page. Whenever we encounter emotional response to any of the thoughts and memories we write about or anything before, our handwriting is affected.

Even though we may know perfectly well how we *would like* to form a particular letter, word, phrase or place it on the page, if a part of our experience of the concept about which we are writing has been traumatic, emotional, or in any way particularly charged, this affects our writing. Even if we are not reacting directly to what we're writing about, we still pass on remnants of our present and past feelings, thoughts, values and sense of self esteem.

These quirky little extras we insert into our handwriting, often unbeknownst even to ourselves, are what make it so fascinating to uncover the mystery of our *hand behind the word.*

3

Beginnings
Starting Out as Handwriting Analyst

No one is really certain exactly when handwriting analysis began as an organized system of study. There is evidence that Aristotle and the Greeks made use of it more than two thousand years ago. The Chinese may have developed their own systems for their version of writing two to three thousand years before that. But certainly in Europe there was little interest in the use of handwriting analysis prior to the nineteenth century. One of the first Europeans to publish on the subject was Dr. Camillo Baldo, professor at the University of Bologna in Italy who in 1622 presented his treatise *Della Maniera di Conoscere in Natura e le Qualità dello Scrittore in una Lettera (A Way of Knowing the Nature and Qualities of a Writer from a Letter He has Written).*

This was his thesis (translated from the quote on page 17):

"For a willing learner, it is possible to understand the thoughts, emotions and disposition of a writer from a sample out of the middle of an intimate letter, providing an astonishing amount of information from a small sample."

Professor Baldo had an interesting idea. Some researchers, scribes and monks followed suit studying these things over the next couple hundred years. But it wasn't until the late nineteenth century that it became a more common subject of academic discussion and research. Certainly not the least of the reasons that handwriting analysis had to wait until the nineteenth century to become more popular was that prior to then the great majority of citizens of the planet did not read or write.

There simply weren't sufficient numbers of writers and readers to be able to do much studying and discussing of anything out in the general world, let alone handwriting analysis. The handwriting which was available was found in fairly formal settings of academia, the church, business correspondence and shipping ledgers. But the man and woman on the street were not generally participants in this formality of daily writing until only the last couple hundred years. That was when it started to get interesting.

No doubt our first handwriting analyst was whoever looked inquisitively or disapprovingly over the shoulder of one of our early writers and said "Interesting that you should write like *that*!"

It's not just that handwriting analysts are all a rather judgmental lot, though there may be some truth to that position as well. But how we write does indeed carry with it a secondary message which we may or may not have intended to include: This is the *hand behind the word*.

An Analyst's Role and Methods

In order to be able to offer their commentary, handwriting analysts must of course be writers themselves or they would not be able to see the patterns. In order to look critically and analytically at handwriting we must be able to look at the details of writing and see more than just letters on a page. In fact, handwriting analysts looking at a message are generally not interested in the text of the message someone writes at all.

What most interests us is how the message lays on the page, how it fits together or fights itself, whether it tickles and dances across the page or slices into the page with venom. We care about what strokes and forms and patterns are used to create the message and which traits or patterns seem to dominate in various sections of the message and page.

As we study handwriting it is important to keep fresh eyes on every sample we see, looking it over very quickly twice: First, as if we've never seen anything like this before. We ask ourselves, "What is the first thing that stands out about this sample?" Then we look it over again and the second time ask ourselves "How is this like any sample I've ever seen before?"

This way, we should be able to respond quickly and immediately to any sample we see. With practice looking, seeing, remembering and comparing samples in your head, you will eventually be able to begin a response to a sample quite literally within seconds of seeing it.

Reference Points in Handwriting

It may sound like a daunting task to think about all that is required to look at a sample, draw upon experience and knowledge and be able to respond to it as both a new piece and a familiar subject. But this will come easily with experience. It is actually only a matter of making some quick comparisons in your mind between some of the minor variations to start the process flowing.

Think of it this way: just as you cannot easily from across the room tell exactly how tall someone is, if you have two people standing together you can easily pick out the taller or shorter of the two. That is because you have an immediate point of reference from which to begin. That makes all the difference.

As you continue your studies of handwriting you will see

more and more samples and you will notice similar patterns and traits popping up again and again. Let those be your points of reference. One of the useful things about looking at people's handwriting is that you generally have right there in front of you one of the best points of reference for the handwriting you are working with: the person who wrote it.

Until you are comfortable with exactly what each trait means, you can use the feedback loop so that you can see and hear when you're on the right track. Talk to the people whose handwriting you are analyzing. Tell them what you think a trait means for their hand, their life. See if they agree.

Developing an Eye to See

This process of studying samples you collect and talking to the writers about what you see in their handwriting will help you to formulate a handwriting analysis system of your own. Study what other handwriting analysts have said, perhaps keep your reference books near until you're comfortable on your own.

As in any other scientific study, once you understand a few reference points, it will become much easier for you to be able to go a little further and further out on a limb and see what you can see. You will test your knowledge as you begin to determine some of the boundaries of the system by which you will be learning.

What is large, for instance? The more you look at variations in size, the clearer that answer will become. You will be able to tell which signature seems oversized compared to the rest of the hand or which indicates a tiny self image from its miniscule writing.

The more you pay attention to slope and form in handwriting the quicker you'll know which sample seems to have a more pronounced downward slope and which has too much distance between letters, or rightward slant.

Eventually more and more of the traits you see will make sense. You will begin to understand them in context of relating to a norm. You will know more about what the various traits mean and how they relate to each other.

Seeing the Overall *Gestalt* of a Hand

Once you are ready to put on your hat as handwriting analyst and start looking at samples, one of the first things you will do is just get a sense for the overall hand by looking at it to sense what it feels like.

That first overall sense of a sample is what we call the *gestalt* of the hand. *Gestalt* is a German word meaning *shape* which is often used in psychology to mean the overall look and feel, the Big Picture. For handwriting, the *gestalt* is a tonal picture and feel of the hand, the perceived overall essence of nature and intensity of the personality. The kinds of questions you'll ask yourself will be these:

How does this hand feel? Is it friendly or intimidating? Is it round or pointed, squeezed up tight or spread out? Is it engaging and appealing or distant and cold? How does it lay on the page? Do I like this hand?

We could answer all of these and more from our perception of the *gestalt* of the hand. Let's look at a couple of samples:

1 2 3 4 5 6 7 8 9 0
1 2 3 4 5 6 7 8 9 0
1 2 3 4 5 6 7 8 9 0
1 2 3 4 5 6 7 8 9 0

I'm redoing my
I'm redoing my
because I didn
tue pen before

What about this first one? What can we say of the gestalt? It's round, rather open, somewhat appealing in that it is friendly but tentative; a bit uptight, discerning, imaginative. It's also self-critical, wounded, tender, confused. I do rather like it; especially the playfulness.

As we turn to this next one, let's ask some other questions: Is it genuine or fake? Nurturing or unavailable? Patient or impatient? Party animal or loner? Intelligent or brainless? Creative or plain?

Gestalt impression of this one: genuine, unavailable, impatient, loner, intelligent, creative. These samples, by the way, are mother and daughter. Can you tell which is which? Probably so, yes?

You will get to where you can look at several traits very quickly within each new sample without even thinking about it. Some of the first traits and strokes which might jump out at you to help give you impressions or the essence of the hand's *gestalt* would be these ten:

1 2 3 4 5 6 7 8 9 0
1 2 3 4 5 6 7 8 9 0
1 2 3 4 5 6 7 8 9 0
1 2 3 4 5 6 7 8 9 0

I'm trying this hand
Thinger again to
like the ballpoint

- Margins (top, bottom, left, right)
- Slant (the vertical leaning motion)
- Baseline (horizontal slope of hand)
- Clarity of form (readable, messy, cluttered, clear)
- Shape, spacing and interplay of the digits
- Pressure (intense, wispy, harsh, feathered)
- Roundness, angularity, shape of the hand.
- Continuity, threadedness, ligature types
- Balance of zones (upper, middle, lower)
- Balance of CAPs and lower case of hand

It would be unusual for you to have to sit down and actually tick through a list like this to get your impressions. But these are where your impressions would likely originate though you would not tend to break it down into such detail. Rather, you would pick up the sample, take a look at it and know almost immediately what you felt about each of them.

Margins (Top, Bottom, Left, Right)

Margins in handwriting tend to relate to our respect for boundaries and rules and the nature of our relationship with the flow of time. In the English writing system, since we write from left to right and top to bottom, the right and bottom of a page represent what is to come in the hand and the left and top tend to represent where we've been.

The left / top is the past and bottom / right is the future. They are sub-divided as well: right-left is generally considered emotional past / future and top-bottom is the action and intellectual past / future.

Where we start a line of digits or a paragraph is a personal statement. We can't always choose where a line will end, but we can choose where it starts. So the top and left margins are the most expressive ones to be looking at for relationship to the past. Right and lower margins express how we expect to meet the future.

Take a look at this illustration. Consider the margins of these miniature pages and let's exaggerate some of the statements about them for the sake of illustration. Take them with a grain of salt since they're exaggerations but you'll get the basic idea of each margin's overall story.

For starters, think about the aesthetics of why we have margins in the first place. What are they doing? They help set up guidelines, expectations and boundaries for our communication.

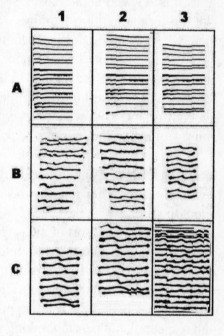

Writers who are mindful of keeping relatively even margins around the page are considered more polite, courteous, respectful. In the illustration, the one with the most even margins would be A3. C1 has three nice margins, too, with an extra large one on top. That's a different kind of message. It is a respectful one which says, "I defer to you" and is the kind of way we might defer to a dignitary or an important business contact. Or perhaps how we might write Thank You notes or condolences for a funeral, that kind of thing. It's a sign of respect, like bowing to the reader.

Not so, B3. That is a little much. If a wide top margin is bowing to the reader, you might wonder if B3 is maybe doing some kind of Native American ritual bowing to the four compass points? But no, I don't think so. It's more likely a lonely self-focused person who wants to make a statement of being special, yet is paralyzed by self-doubt and fear.

It is also a radical waste of paper, which is a part of why it doesn't win any points for respect. C1 says "I respect you so much that I hereby sacrifice a third of my page in your honor."

But B3 says, "Paper? Get over it. It's only paper. If you really cared for me you'd know that I am so sensitive I can hardly stand it. The world is too much for me, so I really need to wrap myself carefully in large protective margins."

It is A3 who is the most respectful and balanced of writers. Not too formal, not too familiar. Just keeping in the middle road there where things are nicely laid out with order and respect.

A1 is an example of someone who is huddling in the past and hesitant about the future. Like a sheep's way of seeing a fence which isn't still in front of them, these folks just can't quite get comfortable with what's to come. But they're great archivists about feelings of the past. Just ask.

Then A2, they're just the opposite. Early adopters of technology always running headlong to tomorrow to fix anything and everything. They have almost no interest in feeling or talking about the past. What past?

B1 and B2 are sort of alter-egos of A1 and A2. B1 starts out with the regular panache and aplomb of a well-balanced being and then somewhere in mid-stream starts to get a bit fearful and doubting and retreats to the comfort of the familiar left margin of the past. Then B2 is just the opposite. It starts out all dignified and respectful, but gets to thinking about what is to come and can't help itself. It just takes off and "Forward ever, backward never!"

Can you guess which two of the nine would be considered the most rude? Which would seem the least respectful of margins?

As you've probably guessed, C2 and C3. C2 is actually one with two combined traits, but they're similar. First, the wide lower margin says they never quite get around to taking responsibility. They're happy to tell you how they used to be successful and how you should respect them for what they used to be. It's a bit of a fantasy world here. Then the second trait: notice how C2 crashed the right margin yet didn't write to the bottom of the page? What are they afraid of? Why both push and stop? That seems a little rude. It's common in addiction and alcoholism where they're just waiting for someone to rescue them as they run head-long off a cliff.

Then the other sometimes addictive or rude one would be C3. It could also be that this is just an incredibly fascinating person with all kinds of things going on and so there's never any slowing down to recognize boundaries or rules or margins.

But more often than not, it's just someone who can't stop, doesn't know when to quit, lacks clear boundaries. Whatever the reason, there are no margins there anywhere. So this is one of those people who will take up whatever space you'll give them. Staying until you kick them out; talking on the phone until you finally say, "Look, I have to go!" spending too long in the shower because they got lost dreaming about all the things they're going to accomplish one day when they finally get out of the shower!

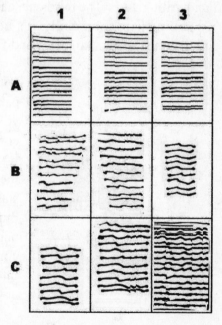

Those who have to practically touch all four margins usually tend to be narcissistic and overly self-focused. That's not unlike the one with those huge protective margins. It's just the other end of the spectrum. These would generally be labeled the intense and emotionally needy side of the bipolar moodswing. They have to tell you everything and it all has to come out now. The other one with the big margins is the opposite pole. They're the type who sigh a lot and feel misunderstood. They just look at you with sad eyes and always seem like they are about to cry.

Slant (the Vertical Leaning Motion)

Slant is a continuum running from back to the left to *forward to the right*. You might think of it similar to the way a person leans into a conversation you're having. When handwriting is like the top one below or further to the left even, leaning back to the left, it is as if someone would be leaning back away from you. Your experience of that kind of a conversation would probably be that the person is likely distant, aloof, cold. That's what it means in handwriting, too. The third one leans back just barely so although it's still perhaps a bit chilly, it's not as distant as the first. The middle one stands straight up and feels perhaps a little stiff.

When we get over to the bottom one and beyond, the person would be leaning way into you to where you'd feel almost cornered, pressured, antagonized. It's a little too intense just as the first is too distant. The more standard lean is the second and third from the bottom. That's a natural lean for conversation and communication: slightly forward, interested, present. Not too aloof, not too weirdly intense.

Baseline (Horizontal Slope of Hand)

Another continuum trait: Baseline or slope refers to the horizontal placement of the hand across the page. Here are five different views of a baseline's motion.

#1 tends to be the basic writing we aim for in order to be normal. Its message is one of stability and presence.

#2 creeps up a bit when we get excitable or optimistic about things.

#3 goes up more quickly like this when we are on a mission, determined, opinionated, captivated or activated by whatever it is we're writing about.

#4 happens when we're moody or medicated or our mind is wandering.

#5 often happens when we're down and depressed.

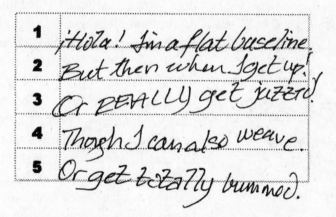

Baseline applies to digits, too. Notice the baseline in the digit sets from the four handwriting samples a couple pages ago. There is some parallel in the baseline of the digits and that of the writing.

Clarity of Form (Readable, Messy, Cluttered, Clear)

Clarity is one of those subjective traits which you will come to appreciate. Samples can vary greatly as to whether they are clear and readable or not. Overall, clarity and form are considered important features for any hand. Here's a couple of examples of lack of clarity.

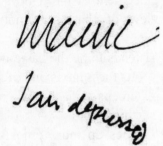

They are further instructive, too, in that a manic hand can often be oversized and loud like this and a depressed hand can be tiny and downwardly sloped. Does either of the two bipolars seems more clear or readable to you?

Shapes and Interplay of the Digits

Shape and interplay of the digits is something which you'll want to be able to take a look at in any *JAQS* sample you receive. The digits are a particularly useful part of the sample because they are so completely translatable between samples. When you have rows of digits all lined up on a page, you have a good relative reflection of margin patterns, size, pressure, speed, baseline, angularity and more. Especially when there are multiple writers in the sample as here, you can see who is more cautious, who listens well, who's controlling, who's optimistic, creative, stable, proud, etc. As you first look over any *JAQS* sample you will notice the way the digits intermingle or stand apart, the way they have full form, or are abbreviated. Digits will be a microcosm of the entire hand.

Pressure (Intensity of the Hand on the Page)

Pressure is something we'll notice fairly quickly in a hand. It doesn't always work well for faxes, photocopies or pictures like these in the book to tell you much about pressure. You can get some idea just by seeing how intense it appears on the page, how dark, how overstruck. But by far the best way to get a sense of pressure is to turn the page over and feel the back of it. You'll get it immediately. Pressure has to do with health and intensity of spirit, commitment, drive.

Roundness and Angularity

Some handwriting is very round, which is indicative of emotion. Some is very sharp and angular which tends to mean action, intensity and passion. Either one of these can be positive or negative. For balance, we like to see a mix of the two in a hand. We sometimes also refer to them in terms of the elements water and fire, which we'll talk more about in Chapter Twelve. Sometimes a water hand will be oversized, like #4 and #5 above. Sometimes a fire hand can seem to slice out of its place, too, like #5 here.

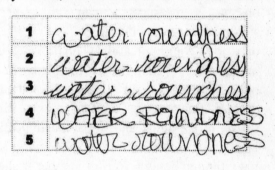

Continuity, Threadedness, Ligature Types

Continuity in handwriting has to do with the way it flows on the page. Does it work? Is it communicative? Does it flow evenly? Does the form of the handwriting contribute to an ease of reading it or does it impede it? Ideally, we're looking for clarity and readability. Threadedness is usually an impediment to readability, and can mean very different things. It might mean a quick intelligent writer of vision and ingenuity writing perhaps impatiently. Or if it intentionally threads to obscure a message, it can signify deceptive, misleading or averted communication. The preview of the Air element shows us a couple of examples of threaded writing in #1 and #2. With only a phrase, we can't tell out of context whether it is apt to be deceptive, lazy or just a quick thinker. But in the writing below, this is just a quick and impatient mind flowing by. She quotes Hamlet, *"Whether tis nobler in the mind to..."* She isn't trying to hide, though being so messy, neither is she very kind to a reader.

Balance of Zones (Upper, Middle, Lower)

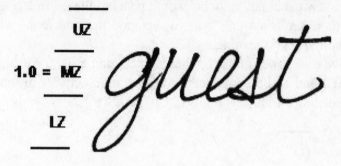

There are three zones in handwriting which we look at. The three zones of handwriting have classical interpretations from long ago. In order to remember some of the basics as to what the zones represent, think of the zones as a kind of metaphor for the human body.

The Upper Zone relates to our spiritual values, religion, ideologies, theoretical belief systems and intellectual curiosity (head, mind and higher thoughts).

The Middle Zone has to do with our basic day-to-day needs and activities, how present we are in our lives and how we behave in the day-to-day action of our lives. Think of it relating to our heart and lungs, torso, strength and action (middle body things).

The Lower Zone is often said to relate to our hidden desires, sensuality and sexuality. It also relates to how we acquire and desire possessions and the finer things in life.

You may wonder how we can use some of these interpretations in the digits since digits tend usually to be middle-upper zone characters. True. They generally have nothing specifically reaching below base. There is a different standard we use for interpreting digits. Even though some writers like this 13-year-old boy have digits drooping into the lower zone, in general we don't treat digits the same way. This would not be a 5 and 6 reaching into the sensual zone; rather it would be a baseline wandering. In digits there are often tails and swoops and tics and loops which have their special meanings.

We make special use of these, since long tails, for instance, in digits tend to be equivalent to lower zone activity in letters. We'll see more about the digits in Chapter Six.

UZ

1.0 = MZ   1234567 89

LZ

In both illustrations of zones, you'll notice that there's a "1.0" by the Middle Zone. That's because whatever is the middle zone becomes the standard: When we speak of size in handwriting, values are usually given relative to the height of the Middle Zone. In the first zones example above, for instance, the tail of the "g" goes below base about 1.5x MZ and the "t-bar" reaches up approximately 0.4x MZ into the Upper Zone. In the digits sample above, the 5 descends into the LZ by approximate 0.4x MZ.

Anytime you see handwriting measurements they will generally be a value relative to an amount x MZ. Even width of letters or digits will be measured in units relative to MZ height. This helps to simplify a sample's measurements if all are given relative to the single measurement standard MZ, or height of the middle zone.

Balance of CAPs and Lower Case of Hand

Ideally, we don't like to see CAPs anywhere in the hand except where capital letters are supposed to show up. There is a kind of hand called the Mixed Case hand which we'll discuss more in Chapter Four. But the basics: CAPs belong in a hand only where they're due: for beginning sentences, for identifying proper nouns or for emphasis and then only as initial letters. Mixing case within a word arbitrarily, just because it wasn't convenient to make a lower case letter there, is not a good reason for using CAPs. The interpretation of mixing case within a word is in most cases quite severe. More about that in the next chapter.

So, to summarize those ten qualities again which you'll be looking at to get the *gestalt* of the hand:

- Margins (top, bottom, left, right)
- Slant (the vertical leaning motion)
- Baseline (horizontal slope of hand)
- Clarity of form (readable, messy, cluttered, clear)
- Shape, spacing and interplay of the digits
- Pressure (intense, wispy, harsh, feathered)
- Roundness, angularity, shape of the hand.
- Continuity, threadedness, ligature types
- Balance of zones (upper, middle, lower)
- Balance of CAPs and lower case of hand

The First Thing that Stands Out About a Hand

When you take a look at a hand to see what stands out first, whatever stands out to you will probably be on the list above. You may not have a specific comment on each trait but you will probably notice something. It could be the sharpness or roundness, slant, slope, an odd way of making some particular letter. What we're looking for is some part of the hand which doesn't fit with the rest. As we seek to understand the meanings of handwriting we are using some unique skills. We are sensing, following, listening to some of the emergent whispers of the hand which tickle us into better understanding the nature of the writer. This is not a hard desperate science with quotas and timelines, percentages and measures which must be precisely calculated.

Understanding or analysis requires more than just an ability to measure and count. It requires that we be able to look carefully enough to discern micro-patterns, shapes, shadows and tendencies with more than just a reductive vision and cold calculated measurement.

Just as geometry requires that we understand the relationship of angles and shapes, so, too, we must understand the relationship between various angles and shapes we see in handwriting. But it is not the measurement of the angles which matters; it is their relationship to each other and to the greater form in which they occur.

How letters or digits are formed and how they link can have subtle variations and yet make a big difference in the interpretation. Our eyes register the difference and yet we often can not describe them in specific terms.

Intuiting Some of the Interpretation of a Hand

In some cases, we will be able to *feel* a part of the answer, almost by merging with the question itself: the handwriting before us. Imagining what it feels like to make a particular character or form will sometimes help us with part of the interpretation.

Perhaps ideally we would be able to compare and contrast this hand with the cultural norm and with every hand we've seen before, keeping everything in perspective. It would be very difficult to process that much information without an enormous storage capacity and time. But our brains do have a powerful relational tool built in, the gift of intuition which offers a way to feel our way to some of the answers, patterns and truths we seek to discover.

Contrary to popular belief, intuition is not foreign to science. It has been an important precursor to many discoveries in science and medicine. Had Einstein not taken the time "to ponder intuitively what it might feel like to be an electron" his Theory of Relativity may have been delayed for years or even decades.

Even though an initial idea or concept may have come from an intuitive "*Aha!*" in a moment of enlightenment or struggling vision, it must then be put to the test of a more cohesive and predictable application with reproducible results and a body of collected knowledge along the way. That is research and science.

In the case of handwriting analysis, two of the primary tools for laying a research foundation for that body of collected knowledge are a personal sample collection and what we call a trait compendium. Our sample collection is the set of samples we personally collect from people in our lives. It provides examples of handwriting from which to learn and, because of the way it was acquired (talking to people), also provides reference contacts to speak with about the traits we may see.

A trait compendium is a personal or a shared reference system of theories and interpretations of handwriting strokes and what they mean. Parts of this book make up a trait compendium, as are other books and reference materials on handwriting. You may also have a personal trait compendium in the form of index cards or collected notes or computer files or writings about your theories and findings related to handwriting you have seen.

A trait compendium is generally compiled by correlation of repeated observations of particular traits within a sample set, theories as to what these traits might mean, and discussion with the writers of the samples to confirm or dismiss the validity of the theory. Those which continually pass validation become the trait compendium on which new research and theories can be based.

Growing Your Handwriting Analyst Within

Handwriting analysis isn't something you'll major in, or even study in school, although it touches several different disciplines. It is psychology, sociology, science, speech, art, even geometry. It has at its core a calling to pay close attention to some of the finer details of interaction and life, trying to make sense of the interrelated discourse. It is theory and applied science and yet it is also mythology and mystery, a fascinating interweaving of observation and discussion.

Whether you think you come to this book just out of curiosity or out of a committed interest to learn and grow and develop a new vision of your world, I suggest that we have crossed paths now for a good reason. It's no accident that you came to be here now reading this. Perhaps one of your seeking interests is to learn, to grow, to share with others in your life. I like to think so.

Hello!
Ask me about your
Handwriting
My name is:

LX

" The Hand Behind the Word "
Handwriting Analyst in Training
© 2005 LLX Press

When you decide to take your interest in handwriting to the next level, there are ways to speed things along even more. As you start talking to people about handwriting and they see you have an interest in learning more about it, you may want to make yourself a little button which says *"Ask Me About Your Handwriting!"* not only as an invitation to writers but as an affirmation to growth.

Taking the Risk to Grow

You will find that as you open to hearing their questions, people will start asking you question after question as they offer you their handwriting. For some, you will immediately be able to offer ample reflection; for others you may have little to say. Tell them you are learning. Ask for their help in learning about their handwriting. The important thing is that you begin. Handwriting wants to speak to you. Try and listen to its messages.

Even if you have apprehensions about your ability to know how to read handwriting, realize that all learning starts with beginners. Every maestro had doubts, regardless of what the early music sounded like. Trust that with commitment, research and continued collection of samples, you will learn and grow enough to share. Asking for people to ask something of you is a great way to grow. The risk of doing so takes you out of your comfort zone where you will learn even more.

Once you declare yourself open to talking about handwriting with people in your daily life, your views of things may well change. Depending on how busy your day is, how many people you see and how interested you are, you could be asked to look at someone's handwriting a few times a week to perhaps several times a day. Certainly people are interested in these things. One thing you will learn early on is that people never tire of hearing about themselves!

Behind the Walls and Façades

Handwriting always has its stories to tell of who a person is, their history, what burdens they bear, what façades they hide behind. It occurs to me that it offers sometimes a bridge, sometimes a wall, like a palace on an island in the waters of who this person is.

It has its façades and its flags, its arches and windows, its dark hidden hallways, its doorways and gates; its moat and its sentries, its turrets and cannon, its drawbridge and chains hold back certain traits. The message in the depths of handwriting's expression spans a wide breadth of the writer's personality. It's the goings and the comings of the business of the day. It's the closets of deceit and the tales of yesterday; the hopes for future's callings and the fears of what might be; the skills and talents known and not, the traits of artistry.

There's really very little in that palace of someone's handwriting which is hidden if we look closely enough. Though the palace guard, the ego, might stand before us smiling, if flames and arrows of another kind fling at us from the handwriting, then the palace walls have fallen anyway. This is not a smile.

Or if the person before us has a kind of impatience and harshness, yet the hand tells a tale of a quiet gentle being just reserving a part of self from the crowding masses, then we won't so much worry about the defensive posture. It's just a mask used to get by. No reason to take it personally.

Uses of Handwriting Analysis

Most people seem to realize that there might be some other kind of information hiding there in the intricacies of handwriting other than just the written message. But they have no idea yet what handwriting analysis is or why they should even think about it. They seem to be asking, *"Of what use is it to me?"*

Handwriting analysis can be a very interesting study, a useful skill to acquire for learning more about the nature of personality, whether our own or someone else's. As long as we have a reasonable amount of handwriting– like a couple sentences and some digits and preferably a signature– many varied aspects of a personality are likely to emerge.

We can see intelligence, artistry, sensitivity, honesty, motivation, sincerity, talents, ambitions, fears, aspirations and a whole host of other traits from a relatively small sample. But it does require more than just a signature or a tiny scrawled note.

Anyone who claims to be able to provide you two or three pages of analysis from only a couple words and no digits written on the back of a photograph or napkin should probably rightly be seen as overstepping reasonable bounds of what is possible with handwriting. But given a reasonable sample, worlds open up as you will see from this book's stories and examples. As to some of the ways handwriting analysis is most useful:

Dating, matchmaking and singles events can provide handwriting analysis at mixer functions to offer compatibility readings for couples who want to see if they might be a match for each other. Handwriting used this way can at best offer couples comparative personality profiles or at least some interesting conversational ice-breaker topics.

When a particular popular personal ad or dating profile has an overwhelming number of mail-in responses, we can also put handwriting analysis to work sifting through a pile of letters to whittle it down efficiently by just looking at the handwriting of the letters. Sometimes we don't even have to open an envelope to know immediately that this one should probably be skipped over or seriously considered.

Psychologists can work with handwriting in one-on-one and group counseling sessions to help get to deeper issues in clients' lives by examining handwritten messages about topics they discuss or about related life issues.

Human resource and training teams can better understand themselves and others by learning about the discrepancy between what they write on a presentation whiteboard and what subtle messages the handwriting there may convey. Taking the time to learn about and consider handwriting's secondary message helps presenters to stay on-target with their intended message instead of unintentionally distracting an audience in a completely unrelated direction when they use handwriting on a class writer board.

Vocational counselors working with job seekers can help to match people with jobs or professional studies based on talents and interests which show up in their handwriting. Sometimes a job seeker may already know of their most prominent talents which will show up in their handwriting; sometimes they don't.

Using Handwriting in the Workplace

Perhaps the most controversial use of handwriting analysis is its use in job screening where an applicant's skills and talents are sometimes reviewed by a handwriting analyst instead of using only a resume, curriculum vitae or personal interview.

Using handwriting analysis like this, an employer can save tens of thousands of dollars in training costs by helping to ensure that a candidate and position are truly a good match before hiring. But workplace handwriting is certainly not without its detractors.

On the positive side, handwriting can emphasize a candidate's skills for music or writing, people management or sales, research, investigation, travel, accounting, interpersonal communication or any one of a number of talents, traits and abilities. Skills of all kinds: mental, emotional and physical, known and unknown can show up to strengthen a candidate's qualifications. The applicant may therefore be delighted to be able to broadcast many new skills from their handwriting which might otherwise not be apparent from the resume or job history.

But the story the handwriting tells won't stop there. It could also be used to unscrupulously, unnecessarily and unethically look into traits and secrets in an applicant's life which the company has no business knowing.

Other things which the sample might also broadcast could be exactly the kinds of things a candidate might be trying to hide, even if they are trying very hard to make healthy life changes: alcohol and drug dependencies, trouble showing up to work on time, temper problems, difficulties with authority and control, certain other "proclivities" which might raise a curious eyebrow in the hiring manager's back room.

Chapters Eight and Ten deal more with the ethics of handwriting analysis and its use in the workplace.

The Big Picture of Handwriting Analysis

Handwriting analysis is both personal and interpersonal. It provides a personal reflection for us to learn from our own handwriting and interpersonal reflection for us to learn from the writing of others. Handwriting is an active present reflection of its writer and the moment in which it was created. It is a kind of a riddle or puzzle to solve, presented with only a few clues.

Something we don't always think about: every sample of handwriting we see every day has behind it a writer with a history, a personality, a set of values and beliefs, all of which were poured quietly and directly into the sample at the moment it was created. That sample was also influenced by the entirety of that writer's life up to that point and whatever experiential and emotional winds blew through that life for better or worse.

There is usually a kind of stardust essence within these hidden ingredients poured into a message: something intangible which causes a tiny vibrating sense within us to send up a flag or two of feelings or emotions, memories or responses we may have when we first see— not read— any handwritten message.

It is important to consider the difference between seeing and reading a sample. Reading takes into account the intended content of a message. But beware! It could be just delaying propaganda put there by a writer trying to give you a reason not to come in, not to see the real jewel of the handwriting. For handwriting analysis you typically won't read a message at all, but will instead look more closely to see the atom of the words: its form on the page.

Trust the writer to have built a bridge to you there, set an entryway before you. Looking deeper, there is always a doorway in if you can find it. Perhaps obvious, perhaps not. But it's there somewhere, an invitation to come in and share with the person before you who reached out, offering a *hand behind the word*.

4

Saints and Criminals
Some Special Views of Handwriting

One of the most common things I hear from people about their handwriting is "Sometimes I write neatly and other times my handwriting is a mess. It varies so wildly! So what does that say about me? Do you think I am destined to be a serial killer?"

Probably not. Certainly there might be some indication in your hand that you could become a serial killer but the mere tendency of a hand to vary a bit from sample to sample or line to line isn't the indication we might be looking for. In fact, you may want to take some solace in the fact that most psychotics have handwriting which is quite consistently psychotic from day to day, hour to hour, sample to sample.

Take a look at the sample on the facing page. We might consider it borderline. The writer of this sample says he was just kidding. When I told him it looked like he had a bit of weird energy there (and not just from the word "aggression") he said no, that he was just messing around. I would warn that it's probably not a very good idea to even pretend that this would be your handwriting. A hand like this would almost certainly be cut from consideration for many jobs, joking or not. I would certainly hope you'd never hire this person for child-care, bookkeeping or air traffic controlling.

Those are jobs where we would not look to a psychotic to take care of things. Although it may not be totally over the edge, this hand appears to be borderline at best. No doubt there's some intensity here. So you might consider hiring a hand like this as a gardener or laborer or maybe a bar bouncer as long as you don't provide any weapon or tools to swing, or people to swing at. But don't expect this person to be a paragon of loving kindness, compassionate caring or accountability.   It's just not there.

There is too much anger and control here, (the sharpness of the hand; the snowball 8's, the totally aberrated 'aggression') and a fairly short fuse (the small too-far-right loop of the 6, the closed "e"). There are also some odd sexual proclivities as evidenced by a combination of the excessive "y" tail and those odd sinister hook (sinister doesn't mean evil; it means leftward) "f" strokes. If he's truly playing, then he learned it somewhere. He's doing too fine a job of imitating trouble.

So, it's not variability or even messiness we'd look at in a hand to make any determination as to whether the writer might be a little "off the deep end of the pond." Not only that, but just because you think your handwriting seems to shift a bit from sample to sample, we might not even agree with you that you're so deviant! Deviance, after all, is relative. It usually is based on the distance (deviation) from a cultural or social norm. First, it is always important to define that norm.

The Paranoia Principle

Many people tend to get a bit overly concerned about their own handwriting when they look at a book like this. They start to see a part of their handwriting in every negative trait we cover. By the end of the book, they've gotten more than a little paranoid. But please, bear in mind that all these traits are relative and it's always a matter of degree. Just because you see a tiny trait in your hand similar to what you see in the book, don't jump to conclusions.

Most of the examples in this book are fairly rare. It's just that the best teaching examples tend to be extremes of the traits, even though they may be very rare out in the world. Don't worry too much about your handwriting unless you start showing up in multiple examples of problem areas and are almost exactly like the examples presented.

By far the largest proportion of the samples we see in real life will be far less interesting, far less intense and far more normal than the samples you see here. Most will be neither Saints nor Criminals but just normal people in their normal lives.

It should be fairly easy to differentiate between Saints and Criminals in handwriting, though who spends their day collecting samples from either? I believe I have seen the handwriting of a couple of saints, though, and definitely have seen the handwriting of some criminals. Not surprisingly, the saints' handwriting is usually easier to look at. It is more pleasant to the eye, respectful in its ability to communicate a special connection with the world and it just feels good.

Let me show you a saint here. See if you don't think this looks like saintly handwriting, even if you don't pay attention to the text. This one is a fine hand with beautiful lilting strokes, a high minded form with a great deal of hope and love and charity built into it. I think you'll agree that her handwriting is a lot more saintly than most we've seen. It has a beautiful fullness to it, living in the present (the middle zone) and reaching up to spiritual Values and the ideal (upper zone). Very lovely hand.

God is Love
He loves you
Love others as
He loves you
God bless you
Mu Teresa mc
1-1-82

In stark contrast to our saintly hand, look at the one below. It is that of a convicted sex addict, a social deviant whose daily existence consists of figuring out when and where his next anonymous sex encounter will occur. Notice the excessively loopy, hooked and misshapen characters, the strange hook / loop"l" in "early" and the convoluted shape of his complex "a". Also note the tiny cramped numbers, especially the 1's and 2's, which confirm his low self-esteem and his inability to relate normally to people.

1234567890
1234567890
of my early day

Perhaps one of the most troubling parts of this hand is that his 7 is the highest and largest of his numbers and has an upper left opinionation tic in it. These suggest that he perceives himself to be a model of principle for others and doesn't seem to understand that there's anything out of the ordinary about his principles. In fact, he even sees himself as a leader. This could be a bit of a social concern, but for the fact that it's all fantasy; there's no leadership trait in his hand anywhere. He's delusional, quite in denial of his problem.

The huge loops in his "y's" and their downward terminal stroke suggest an uncontrollable sexual desire. Although he has no sense of responsibility or awareness of the world (no middle zone, a 0 open at the top, a very sharp, flippant 2) his compressed and excessively looped "a" and "d" suggest that he lies a lot, perhaps to hide his addiction from others? His wandering baseline in both words and digits tells us of his instability. Even in so small a sample as this, we get a picture of a rather confused, troubled and tortured soul.

The tiny size of his numbers in relation to the letters on the page are an indication of his alienation and withdrawal and his lack of ability to control his desires. That hole in the top of his number 0 suggests a disconnection from Spirit and a Higher Power. There is no consistent upper zone in his hand; they're all messed up and convoluted. It would be nice if he would take to heart the message on Mother Teresa's sample. It was she who was the writer of the saintly hand from the previous page.

Now to another of my favorite saints, here is Abe Lincoln's hand. I believe he qualifies as a saint. I love his handwriting. Can't you just feel his essence emanating from this sample?

I have a sample of his Gettysburg Address on the wall of my office because I think it's a beautifully expressive hand. When I say it is a saintly hand, I don't mean it's perfect or that he always followed all the rules of the elementary copybook or the examples at the top of our blackboard in fourth grade. But look at the flow in this hand. Look at the basic form. Isn't it poetic and beautiful? It has such an elegance about the way it gently flows.

We can tell that he was meticulous and quiet. Even though he was a very tall man, (which, no, we can't tell from the handwriting) he would have been soft spoken and very gentle. I especially love the way he wrote the word "Liberty." We can *feel* his concept of Liberty from that word. To him it was a fragile ideal, a gift which we must never take for granted. He calls upon our willing vigilance and offers us a nurtured loving hope. I see caution in the "L," hope in the "b," a resigned commitment to move forward in the "ty" and a delicate trust and faith in that perfectly placed "i" dot.

Lincoln's Liberty is a very beautiful word, in every sense. I don't know if there is a better example in this book of just what we mean by seeing the *hand behind the word*. I always find it an honor to be able to gaze upon the writing of Abraham Lincoln and understand this incredible man: statesman, friend, husband and father. From just this tiny portion of the hand we can glean a great portrait even a hundred and fifty years after his death. That is the power of handwriting's gift to be able to communicate across miles, years and lifetimes.

A Three Year Social Chronology in Handwriting

Meanwhile, back at the criminal side of things: I offer you a set which has at its core a story of guile and deception. This time I let the digits alone tell this real-life story in the making. I learned the details several years after the fact, though I had been taking handwriting samples along the way.

During the times I saw this man, I had before me what seemed a pensive and intelligent hand, for the most part well-mannered and kind. I could tell something was out of the ordinary, but every time I'd bring up some oddity about his hand, he never talked much. Rather, he was mostly evasive and jolly. His hand is what I might call a "let me hide and not show you who I am" type of writing, quite different from what we've seen in other samples.

The writer is a man in his mid-thirties sampled over a three year period, from the time he was growing more and more unsure how to keep some of his secrets from his friends, family and the law. The top row is the first summer. Something was upsetting his baseline and emotional stability. Notice the way the digits' horizon trails off downward. He's not in a very stable state. He's worried, maybe depressed, seems a little stressed and on edge by the way the 6 is kind of flat. 2 seems to be avoiding getting much involved with people. Notice it has no loop on the bottom, only a sharp corner, and the top hook seems to start a bit late, almost at the top instead of over to the left and down a bit as it normally would. All of these things point to tension.

1234567890
1234567890
1234567890

What I learned later is that at this time, he was in turmoil about the inappropriate relations he was having with a young son and daughter of one of his colleagues from work. As his handwriting reflects, he was experiencing complications within a major trauma in life. Notice the 8 (sense of major traumas) has a tangled confusion atop it, suggesting a crisis in his world. Then, his 1 (sense of self) shows an identity loss and lack of self worth. Normally his 1 is taller than any other digit and stands firm. But here his 8 is paramount and the 1 is small, barely there, almost hiding as it hovers unusually close to the distant cold 2.

His 4 (intimate relations and sexuality) is bent and skewed and leans backward. There's some kind of pressure there. His 7 (sense of principles) is definitely asking some questions, knowing something is wrong. Look how troubled is its flow on the top.

Between just that 7 and 8, I'm sure I must have said something to him at the time. It would probably have been something akin to "Something's going on here in your sense of principles which is causing you a bit of a tangled drama in life. What's up there?" No doubt he did not answer me.

The 7 is malformed and uncomfortable. It is reflective of someone on the edge of a challenge of principles. Notice there is a trailing off on the top left edge of the 7 where normally you'd expect a full solid stability with follow-through.

By the next summer (middle row) we can tell that he's tried to deal with things by pushing forward (slant of all digits) and has made a concerted effort to declare improved self-image. Everything is tightened up and firm. The 1 seems very powerful and confident. Perhaps too much so. It doesn't fit. His 1 is taller and more usual for him but notice also the exaggerated thickness of the 1's staff and the way it stands away from the 2. It's a bit defiant and a bit too cocky and confident. It seems to say, "Me? Lack of confidence? No, No, I'm fine." Reminds me of Shakespeare's *"Methinks thou dost protest too much!"* It all seems a bit thick.

4 and 7 (intimate relations and principles) are also a bit pronounced. More defiance. Later chronology shows that this was a time when he was still offending and so may have had reservations about giving this sample or relating to people (distance between all digits) because he was trying to live in a distant private world. His digits are almost all smaller and tighter than normal, except the defiant ones. The 8 still registers trouble in its complex tangle at the top, though less obvious. His role in the world at his job (9) has suffered and is compressed to where there is almost no "world" loop left in the 9's top.

By the third summer (bottom row) he has withdrawn and pulled in even more (notice the narrowness of the row). He also realizes there may be trouble in his relations (4). Look how tiny the 4 is. His 8 is also tiny so he's compressed his sense of major traumas in his world. He appears to be in denial that there is any trauma there, though he may be about to blow: the 8 still registers the tangle and complexity. The small 5 has a nervous squareness in what normally would be a round lower loop (sense of humor and time). Compare it with the other two 5's from the two previous years. His 0 in this year's sample (sense of the world) reaches

1234567890
1234567890
1234567890

more and more counter clockwise to close its loop. He is thinking of his world in terms of where he has been and how he is affected now by his past.

His 3 in this last sample is very strong and full, with a nice rocker base on it. That suggests that he's amiable and friendly, even though he seems too up-tight. He must have at this time been a good hard worker, going above and beyond the call of duty. Even so, though, his sense of reputation and self in the world (his 9) is very tiny and tenuous. Something was amiss here.

What turned out to be the case was that Children's Services began investigating him so he abruptly quit his job and ran away, eventually to be permanently on the run in another country and in hiding. I don't know exactly what happened or where he is today, but these are the last samples I have of his before he quite literally became a fugitive several years ago.

Clearly there was something up in his handwriting for years. That I could see. But until I heard details from others as to what had been going on, I could not tell what it was. I could only tell it was a trauma of intimacy, self-image and reputation in the world.

Now that I have heard more details of the situation, I look back and wonder why he was giving me samples at all? It occurs to me that perhaps he kept giving his sample in order to know if I could see into his situation, or if he could still count on being invisible. That cloak of invisibility is one which abusers and other criminals will rely on most in order to not get caught.

In handwriting as in other parts of life, things are not always what they seem. All through this man's hand, we see a neat and ordered hand. It always felt polite and well-mannered, kind and mostly pleasant on paper. Clearly there were oddities in the hand. But his careful distance and aloofness when we spoke and his tendency to evade with jovial asides didn't help me to get to any truth of the matter in his hand. Some con men are very good.

I don't know if I would have ever been able to nail it exactly without hearing the real story to fill me in. But it is a very interesting hand if for no other reason than it otherwise seems so normal. Something kept gnawing at me about it, but just what, I wasn't sure. It's a good example to help us see why we sometimes need to ponder the traits in a hand in order to make sense of it.

The Mixed Case Hand

On now to a trait which isn't exactly Saintly or Criminal. But nonetheless it is a trait we don't consider positive or like to see. It occurs with fair regularity, however, in all sorts of hands all the time. People who have it may otherwise seem rather normal. What is the trait?

It's that of mixing full-formed capital letters with lower character text in the middle of the same word. Following here is one example of what the Mixed Case hand can look like. (By the way, this one also has the "looks like it was written with a razor blade" trait. His is a fiery intense personality with a very sharp mind). Sometimes there are fewer CAPs than lower case letters; sometimes just the opposite.

It most often occurs in men's handwriting, possibly because it tends to be related to competitiveness and intensity being cranked

1234567890 1234567890

1234567890 1234567890

I would That I could
But I don't so I'm Not.

6081597:2316

up a notch or two too high, and fear of loss of power and control. When stressed, these people often tend to have loud voices and laughter and feel a need to dominate a conversation if they can. CAPs tend to magnify the intensity of a hand. They yell out their point saying, "Look at me! I am here! Don't forget me!"

From a company's standpoint, perhaps it can seem to be a perfect hand for a salesman because these people can often be almost ruthless about pursuing leads and making sure they get heard. Of course this could backfire for the company since, from a customer or co-worker perspective, these people can seem bullyish, annoying and far too competitive. It's that power and control thing again, like snowball 8's on steroids.

When I see mixed case in people's hand I sometimes offer some unsolicited reflection about power and control, suggesting that perhaps they haven't thought that one through all the way:

> *Consider that it is not so much control you seek*
> *as freedom from someone else's control.*

That's a big difference. If they can have an "*Aha!*" about it, perhaps they can tone down a notch or two, maybe dim the CAPs to lower case at least most of the time. Making these changes in handwriting can help lower stress and change a life. Really.

Certainly handwriting is much better off if you can use CAPs only for emphasis and capitalization. They are just not necessary for yelling; they don't add to the aesthetics of a hand.

Over-use of CAPs suggests a willingness to crash boundaries and break rules, to win at any cost. It's a sign of over-competitiveness

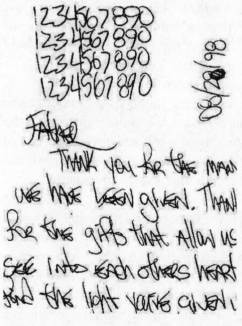

and is often found in the hand of sales people and hucksters whose ethics aren't always the most admirable.

Here is another example of mixing case, this time from a writer who wants to be a spiritual leader. He is a young man in his early-thirties with a youthful artistry and a charismatic charm about him. When you meet him he would smile and you would probably think him a gentle guy which he does seem to be for the most part.

But you might also sense a discomfort and nervousness in him. It shows up in his hand as some troubling traits.

The word "Father" which is the focal point of this prayer is ironically rather tough to read because of a convolution of the "a" and "e" complicating his hand. The way he stabs the "e" with a painful extra stroke every time takes away its base, giving the "e" nothing to stand, making it lopsided and apt to tilt. An "e" is usually about communication. This kind is a combative non-communicator.

There is also another quite troubling trait in this hand called the "claw d / b." It shows up at the end of the word "find" and the beginning of the word "been." See  the pointers in the illustration at the right. Similar to a felon's claw, the claw d / b is about identity confusion and deception. It would be especially unwarranted, unlikely and troublesome in a church leader's hand since it often indicates a tendency toward anti-social behavior, anger, violence and cruelty. This is certainly not how we usually think of a church leader. So either he's not really a church leader or this church has some trouble brewing.

If we look into his digits, we see in the 2's a genuine desire to connect with people (that extended tail to the right) and in the 3's a fairly strong commitment to go above and beyond the call of duty in his work and neighbor relations (a good rocker base on the bottom of the 3). These seem communicative and positive.

But now look at the 7's. If we were to expect to see here a principled man of religion, it would seem to follow that he would have strong and well formed principles (7's) but his 7's are wobbly and malformed. No angle on the top right anywhere to be seen.

That top right angle on a 7 is something we need to see in order to be convinced that this person has good boundaries and awareness of principles. The size of the stem or vertical bar in the 7 relates to the sense of "I" in principles, a willingness to commit and hold one's word. In his 7's, the stems are irregular and inconsistent. This isn't a good sign for principled values.

He is also a right-handed writer with a markedly sinister or leftward slant to most everything except the number 9. His 9 is well leaning to the right as we might expect for someone motivated and interested in learning and growing in a profession. The 9 represents the sense of vocation, calling, reputation. At least he believes he is on a mission and seems committed to moving forward. That counts for something.

But with the combination of the overall sinister slant and the irregular form of most of the digits, unfortunately this doesn't bode well for being the handwriting for a spiritual leader. Although he sees himself as a leader, he probably has a way to go before people seek him out much or trust him.

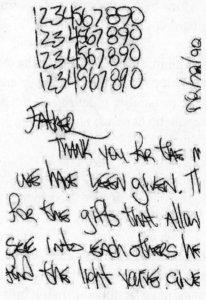

There's one more mystery: why did he stand the date on its ear? Another eccentricity, as if to say, I am a stranger to my day; no one understands me. There was no shortage of room on this page for him to put the date horizontal, yet he chose to stand it on its ear, perhaps to add to the drama of his sigh we sense in the hand.

In his signature (which is not included here for privacy's sake) we see a giant circle around his first name, which is rather odd in itself. Signature circles usually surround the last name or the entire name, but not usually the first name. It usually is a clannish "keep-it-in-the-family" type stroke, with narcissistic overtones. Certainly when it's the first name it is very narcissistic. It screams, "See me! I exist! Really I do!"

This, with the sinister lean of the entire hand suggests a confused and troubled young man who feels people just don't understand him.

When we compare this hand with Mother Teresa's we get an immediate contrasting idea about spirit and religion and leadership. We begin to easily see how the container from which spirit pours really matters. The vessel will always add a flavor of its own to the spirit which pours forth from out that chalice.

I could not say definitively that this man is any less capable of being a spiritual leader than any other. But certainly the vessel in which he carries spirit differs from Mother Teresa's. His seems to be a chalice yet becoming, a vessel not quite made. Perhaps it is a vessel of fear, hesitation, self-judgment and difficulty in seeking in its way. Whatever the case, it is unlikely he is yet ready for leadership in the church. Many blessings to him as he opens to the possibility of spirit and finds himself and a path homeward. May he be at peace and find comfort at the hand of the Father he invokes.

Although I applaud his desire to learn and grow and share, I could not be led by this man as a spiritual leader. There is too much trauma and unsettled energy there for me to feel comfortable with his ability to lead, especially spiritually.

Seeing the hand of Lincoln, I would follow Abe to the ends of the earth and trust him to guide me well. I would trust Mother Teresa to lead me naked, blind and bound. But this man: No, I would have trouble following him very far for very much at all.

The Anti-Social Nature of the Mixed Case Hand

Whether or not mixed case writers are considered "normal" in their lives, the mixed-case hand is considered an anti-social trait because of its outward flaunting of social norms. Like all anti-social traits it is something we do well to try and grow beyond in our hand and try to replace with a more healthy form.

If you are a mixed case writer, you may want to seriously consider seeking to change that, although it's unlikely you'll be able to change it overnight. You will also want to be aware of the strong likelihood that this trait originated as a psychological issue in your earlier life which affected not only your hand but also the way you deal with people, stress and communication.

The drama and trauma behind your mixed case writing can also be affecting your ability to find or keep a job, to feel understood by your friends and family, to be trusted and loved in a relationship. Mixed case in a hand is almost always present within a context of difficulties in self-esteem, communication, power and control struggles and social confusion. Certainly you are not alone in being a mixed case writer. This is perhaps one of the most common negative traits in the book. But that doesn't mean you cannot overcome it if you choose.

There are varying degrees of intensity with the mixed case hand. It is considered less an intense issue if there are fewer other stroke aberrations with it. The more negative strokes with it, the more troublesome. Take a look at this next image. It is four different mixed case writers at once, with progressively more negative traits from top to bottom:

I am Working At the Coffee
SHould chestmas be
un IMAGE to PoTRAY. ONE THAT
I REAlly DON'T KNOW

The top two certainly are not standard writing. But the way the case is mixed fairly evenly within a stable hand is more acceptable than the lower two, where slant and pressure of the characters varies so much.

The last one has severe addiction issues with alcohol and drugs, which no doubt compromises his writing and adds part of the shakiness and disorder. He also has the felon's claw in his "y," a sign of identity confusion, anger and possible sexual deviance. The third one just above that, has a habit of smoking marijuana every day when he gets home from work. It doesn't help the stability of his baseline and letter form. The second one down is his girlfriend who also smokes marijuana but not as heavily. Her baseline wanders and she has an angry "b," but still would likely be considered more stable than the two below her.

The mixed case hand is more common in men and is perhaps the single most common anti-social trait seen among incarcerated men and women. But we also find it in church leaders, teachers, doctors, lawyers, politicians. In short: it can pop up in most any walk of life.

A strong component set often seen with it include the double snowball 8, exaggerated sense of space in the hand (either super compressed or excessively airy) and a general sense of (loss of) power and control, often with bloating of the digits like 6 and 8 and a confused leaning or slant of the hand. The mixed case hand is not a hand of comfort and ease, nor is it a hand of stability. It is usually quite notorious for lacking in peace and confidence with its uncomfortable oppressed form.

The Generational Hand of the CoCos

The mixed case hand was also a kind of generational hand for what I call the CoCos: Children Of the Children Of the Sixties. This generation includes those born between about 1970 and 1985. The CoCos love their Goth, their sharp wit and cutting retorts for each other. Like all dutiful kids hellbent on showing their parents what's right, the CoCos were a generation dedicated to shaking up everything their hippie parents said and did, most especially everything the parents said should be laid back and left at peace.

Where their parents wore white and made love not war; they wore black and reveled in war games and body piercings. Where their parents had folk music and sandals they had head-banging earbleed and combat boots. Where their parents wrote sickeningly sweet love poetry and dreamt of bliss, they wrote blood poetry from Exacto knife wounds on their own bodies and dreamt of total annihilation of the planet in a big nuclear blast.

Should we be surprised, then, that CoCos should choose for their generational hand a hand of mixed case, which represents in handwriting exactly what so much of the rest of the CoCos Manifesto says? Probably not a huge leap of understanding to be able to see that this dark-side generation needed to wake up their dreamy white cotton parents and bring the darker side of life back into the light. One thing for sure: they certainly succeeded at putting a mixed-case hand on the map of the handwriting analysis timeline!

Even though the mixed case hand may indeed be considered at least borderline anti-social in its general form, many of the CoCos are today quite socially functional and hold positions in society of distinction and merit. Most outgrew the mixed case hand just as most of their parents outgrew the long hair, sandals and white cotton.

It's not just criminals or the CoCos who will have the mixed case hand though between the two they do have a strong proportion among them. It occurs in all generations mostly among those whose anger and frustrations with boundaries and rules say they need to buck against them and break them if they can.

Rebelliousness in writing like the mixed case hand is most prevalent in writers who grew up in a difficult family situation, often struggling against oppression and control issues. Alcoholism, drug and boundary issues may have played a significant role in the writer's need to rebel in order to try to reclaim a sense of boundaries. The mixed case writer often has difficulty in keeping a calm social exterior when things don't go as planned. They often feel a need to respond as loud abusive bullies of communication with a shorter-than-average fuse and a stronger-than-average temper.

If I were a hiring manager when a mixed case writer came in to apply as a teacher in a day care or a caregiver for senior adult living center, or any position where vulnerable personalities might be in their care, I would be *very careful* about whom I selected.

The mixed case hand is a self-focused handwriting of a personality still very much in flux. It is often a temporary state in young adulthood characterized by a reclaiming of power and clarity of personal boundaries. Because of its both defensive and offensive tendency to fly in the face of tradition, rules and social bounds, it is definitely not just "normal."

Although many of the CoCos had it, many of them did not. Even for those who did, it was more a stylistic bravado and fad rather than a true creed. Most eventually outgrew it.

The full-blown mixed-case hand is usually associated with bravado, shortness of temper, impatience, judgment of peers, and control issues which can lead to cruelty and insensitivity especially within the weak or the young.

Be very careful if you see this trait in a babysitter, childcare or eldercare provider, or person in social control. Get references at least twice and if you select one of these as an employee, you may want to keep an eye on video monitors in your facility!

That said, don't rush out seeing only a minor instance of mixed case in someone's hand and have them blackballed or cast out. Of the four samples above, the top one is one I might still hire in most any position as long as he was supervised carefully and monitored for temper.

The third one down is one of the CoCos I actually did hire as a technical services assistant. But he was only working on computers in our lab and not working directly with the public. Over a one

EVERYTHING". I too would like to have an IMAGE to POTRAY. ONE THAT would Be enjoyed by all and most important myself. You Serval BRING OUT THE

year period, both his handwriting and his personality changed. The handwriting from above is when we first met, the lower one from a year later. Believing in him helped him to feel better about himself. His handwriting is still not perfect, but whose is? None of us is a wartless willow!

you've changed my at least perspective quite dramatical for that I say

thank you,

There's probably at least one or two strokes in anyone's hand which could, out of context, be used against us. That is the nature of the complexity and the veracity of handwriting. Unless our handwriting can look like Mother Teresa's it's probably best we don't judge others too harshly. It might come back to haunt us!

If you are looking at someone's hand who has only a couple instances of mixed case in it (especially if it only appears in their signature) then you need to have further proof elsewhere in the hand that this is truly a case of anti-social boundary crashing in order to make such a determination.

Overly Neat Handwriting

One trait which tends to surprise a lot of people when it shows up on the negative side of the ledger is handwriting which is too neat.

But when it seems that a hand is indeed too neat to be real, then it probably is. It is most likely that it is trying to hide something. Having picture-perfect handwriting is not the kind of thing most handwriting analysts are going to expect you to be smiling and proud about.

There are a couple of things here that push my suspicion buttons almost immediately. First, that excessive tail on the 2 and the big gap after it. This would be what we'd call a "Look at me!" stroke. It says "See, I know how to make a perfect 2 and to make sure you see it, I'll leave some space after it." Not that she's even aware that she's making this statement, but that's essentially what it means.

Then the 3: It is a bit of exaggeration; it is too full, too closed. Like the 2, it must have been drawn very, very slowly. Next, the

1 2 3 4 5 6 7 8 9 10

6 and 7 stand out to me as two more very slow deliberate strokes. In the 3 and 7, heavy ink in middle of the right side strokes. And both the shelf of the 3 (center stroke) and the top right corner of the 7 seem a little too tightly angled, trying too hard to be perfect. Another couple of those "Look at me!" strokes.

9 has a bit of excess ink in the upper right because it was slowly drawn there. The 1 of the 10 is unevenly stroked, almost shaky. And the whole row of digits (probably because it was drawn too carefully digit by digit to remember to actually make it a whole set together) is wandering up and down on a very ungrounded baseline.

Having concentrated so much on the formation of each digit she forgot the baseline altogether and the fact that the digit set is a group together, considered at a single line.

You could probably see some of those things in the digits now that they are pointed out. Now let's look at the cursive writing which went with the digits. Surely here you will immediately see there is something wrong? Look at that phrase below.

Bear in mind that this is a middle-aged woman, not a fourth-grader trying to please her teacher in a handwriting class. Do you notice that this handwriting seems a little too perfect?

Good Little Boy / Good Little Girl

It is so slowly done that it's more a drawing than handwriting and can hardly be called writing at all. Its aim and intent is all about image and the need to deceive and distract away from any imperfections. It is far too slow, far too controlled, far too heavily inked along the way. Something is happening here and it's not good. Note how the ink clumps in the places where the slow

Eugene. The music is moving

overstrikes show, like in the "g", "i", "o." The excessively formal (and shaky) cross-bar on the capital "T" is also particularly telling of some problems here.

One of the greatest fears of this writer is being judged or noticed to be anything other than an outstanding achiever and a "Good Little Girl."

That's why we call this kind of writing the "Good Little Boy / Good Little Girl hand." It is not considered an attractive or positive hand, which may surprise some people. Rather, it is a sign of deceit. But why? What is behind it?

The main problem is that it is completely inauthentic. It sets out to hide its flaws. Moreover, it tries to present a completely different image. We'll talk more about this kind of hand in Chapter Ten, under handwriting analysis for people managers.

Very likely, the reason this writer is prone to writing like this is because she grew up in a hyper-vigilant, hyper-critical household where she could never do anything right. Consequently, she became very fearful of being judged for being anything other than the "Good Little Girl."

The word "music" is difficult for me to even look at, especially knowing that this is a middle-aged woman, because it screams out "Please! I want so much to be perfect! I want so much to matter to someone as Good."

Then there's the perfectly placed "i" dots, perfect little hooklet on the "c" as we were taught in 4th grade. But the main trouble with writing like this is that nobody writes like this who isn't trying way too hard to hide. She judges herself very harshly and is very sensitive about her handwriting for some reason.

It is very important to try and be respectful and reflective when speaking to such a writer. She's already very sensitive about her hand so it's important not to say anything to make that worse.

I might tell her that her hand is nice looking but I suspect it's only one that she uses. Perhaps she has another she'd like to show me? That's exactly what happened in this case.

Once we were able to establish an opening to talk about her having "another" hand, I told her this one didn't seem very real. She did give me a second sample, though she also rather objected to not being able to convince me to see the "fancier" one as her primary hand.

Perfection's Message

More often than not, those who write a little too perfect tend to be nervous over achievers who are very eager to hear someone say "My, what a lovely hand you have there!" but that's not what they usually hear.

If we watch while the writer is writing, we will see that it takes too long to write a sample like that, which is one of the first signs tending to give it away as not being authentic.

This second sample was much quicker for her to write and that is no surprise: it is the real hand she uses. She still has the long tail in the final 2 of the date but that's probably because I told her it was one of the things I was looking at. Look at the first 2 in the date; that feels a lot more authentic.

It must be stressed that when we see handwriting that is not authentic, it is not necessarily true that we're dealing with a crook. It could just be a worried over achiever who is trying so hard to make a positive first impression.

But, crook or over achiever, it's often useful for them in the long run to let them know we see their inconsistency. Together we can then perhaps go ahead and get to the bottom of why we're dealing with an inauthentic handwriting sample. There must be a reason. They may be ready to talk about it and they may not. Either way is fine.

1 2 3 4 5 6 7 8 9 10
1 2 3 4 5 6 7 8 9 10
1 2 3 4 5 6 7 8 9 10
1 2 3 4 5 6 7 8 9 10

This feels less real than the other, because my mood was to go with the other. Why can you analyze only the kind

October 23, 1992

Two Quick Tests for Authenticity in Writing

Here are two quick tests for whether a hand is likely authentic:

A) How fast was it written? Watch the sample being written. Taking into consideration the variables owing to age and health and injury or arthritis, etc.: Was this hand written in what seems to be a relatively normal amount of time for the content presented? Was the writer in a natural flow?

B) Are all of the five repetitions of digits within a relatively narrow slice of similarity? Taking in consideration any interruptions in the flow of events during the time the sample was written, is the writer fairly consistent within the four rows of digits and the fifth in the date at the bottom of the page?

0123456789 0
0123456789 0
0123456789 0
0123456789 0

*In spite of even being
my favorite number,
the number* 05/13/03

Let's apply some of what we saw in the last sample to this next one. Here is a sample of a similar situation. This is a slightly younger female writer eleven years later giving me a very similar sample, even with one of the telltale 2 markers. Incidentally, it does seem that women are more apt to give a patently inauthentic sample than men. I have a couple suggestions as to why. Perhaps it's that men are less concerned about their image on paper or perhaps it's the fact that girls in school usually excelled before the boys, so it became a lifelong habit to try and get the gold star?

Interestingly enough neither of these two followed directions. They were given identical directions in the front of the sample book. Yet look at the digits. The first writer wrote "789 10" and this writer put 0's at both ends. Not that it matters for the sample but it is interesting to note that although these two are trying so hard to appear flawless, neither followed simple instructions.

When the young woman above wrote her sample for me I probably said something like, "Hey, thanks for that. Now, if you'd like to show me your real handwriting we can get started!" Although she was rather irritated with me for that, she did give it.

Like the earlier writer, the first thing that gave this away was the 2's. Recall that 2's have to do with the way she deals with impersonal view of other people. The variability she has in those 2's seems a little extreme. Not that she might not have varied impersonal views of people, but not so likely in this short time frame in which the sample was being written. At the time she was writing her 2's she was unaware I'd be saying that they were inauthentic. But no doubt in a couple minutes when she showed it to me, she would be having a pretty consistent view of this impersonal annoying know-it-all in front of her who was telling her that she was misrepresenting her hand.

But look what she did with those 2's and 3's. There are about four different 2's there. Strike one. Then the 3's in the date differ from those above; strike two. But the third strike was even easier: she wrote excruciatingly slowly for the entire time she was writing. Strike three: You're OUT!

Under the circumstances here, it was quite appropriate for her to be writing what she did for that second bout: "Who the hell are you to tell me how to write!?" I wasn't telling her how to

Why in the world do I
care what other people
think? Just who the hell

write; but I was telling her that she wasn't telling me, either. We laughed, though. She has a nice sense of humor and didn't take it personally. Once she offered her real sample, we were able to proceed a little more honestly on both parts.

The Ambidextrous Hand

One interesting variation on handwriting we hear about is from the ambidextrous writers among us who truly have more than one handwriting to use. These are people who can actually write legibly and relatively well with both hands. When they ask which hand I'd like to have them use, I say either one, or both.

Although they are neither Saints nor Criminals, I want to include a couple of these in this chapter because of their potential to help you identify variation. Some artistic ambidextrous forgers for instance, actually do write with their non-dominant hand to perfect their forgeries since their non-dominant hand is often more able to be flexible.

Take a look at this pair. This is a young man in his early twenties, not a forger, but just a writer who writes with both hands. The first is his left hand, the second, his right. As with most ambidextrous writers the two hands seem to have slightly different personalities. But they are both authentically his own. He told me that when he writes with his left, he tends to have more poetic and philosophical thoughts, so that's what he uses it for: as a way to communicate with that part of his being. His right hand tends to be more pragmatic and task oriented, with a signature and several digits that lean right.

Though he is a quiet fellow in the world and is predominantly right-handed, when he writes with his left hand, it's interesting to note that he seems taller, more confident and more spiritually and intellectually curious. His 5's, 7's and 9's reflect this taller self as well. Also note the artistry of his g's and f's in the left hand.

1 2 3 4 5 6 7 8 9 0
1 2 3 4 5 6 7 8 9 0
1 2 3 4 5 6 7 8 9 0
1 2 3 4 5 6 7 8 9 0

But in everything we should have the greatest patience with ourselves and... 8/4/04

Consider the possibility of writing sometime with your own non-dominant hand. An intriguing exercise from split brain studies sometimes used in counseling has our dominant hand write a question and the non-dominant hand answer it. Try it sometime.

A Few More Words on Variations in Handwriting

There are many reasons why writers will have multiple ways of writing. One could be that they are truly ambidextrous and able to write legibly and yet differently with each hand. Or, like the second of the two women above, it could be that a writer's cursive is sometimes completely different from her printing in form, stroke, rhythm and slant. This can feel like a totally different hand, although there are still some link and form similarities if we look very closely.

One of the main reasons writers will have their multiple ways of writing is that neat handwriting often gets more positive attention than bad handwriting gets negative attention. So the net motivation for a writer who yearns for attention is to use the variation between the two to advantage whenever possible.

Where there is no likelihood of benefitting from positive attention, the "messier" writing is used since it isn't messy enough to draw negative attention and the situation doesn't warrant the extra effort required to maintain the "neater" handwriting.

These writers probably learned fairly young that they could get positive attention from many people by writing in an extraordinarily neat manner. They are probably used to getting points for being what we call the Good Little Boy / Good Little Girl, a behavior which likely began years ago way back in early elementary school when they were able to master handwriting and get a gold star for being perfect for that day.

Sometimes the neat handwriting trick is used in some very clever and deceptive ways. Having learned that one way to gain useful attention, trust and reputation is to write very neatly, they set out to carefully do exactly that. It is, however, not so much that they want to stand out as perfect. But they must avoid at all costs standing out as imperfect, flawed or defective.

Having this fragile sense of self, writers who seek to use the neat handwriting lure often tend to believe that in order to get their needs met, they need to work secretly and behind the scenes. In business, for instance, one of the things this is used for is to keep up a ruse of perfection while working some white collar crime behind the scenes which the Good Little Boy or Good Little Girl would never be suspected of pulling off.

This is exactly the realm of the classic embezzler. Most embezzlers would smile and greet you and appear to be the nicest Good Little Boy or Good Little Girl in the department. But what they don't realize is that this is exactly the kind of behavior and handwriting most apt to eventually give them up. More on embezzlers and using handwriting in a specifically business context in Chapter Ten.

What About That Forgery?

Most of us recall stories of kids who forged a parent's signature on notes at school and perhaps was good enough to pass. But forgeries in the real world are usually much more difficult to pass off. Each of us has a very particular method of writing and it's very difficult to be able to get *everything* exactly right with it in order to get reasonably close.

Try it yourself. Pick any sample in the book and try to write exactly like it, keeping slope, slant, size and spacing all the same. Most people will find that it's harder to do than it looks, even for what appears to be a simple sample or one which seems similar to your own.

A truly good forgery is rare, although the forger's business is to draw on the strength of the fact that there are many people who do not look carefully enough to tell.

When we look at handwriting to detect what is authentic and what is not, we are typically looking at more than just letters on a page. One thing we'll look at is where a writer begins a particular stroke, at what angle in what place on the page. Different combinations of letters will begin and form and end strokes differently.

Try it yourself. Take a look at a sample paragraph you've written and notice the different ways you connect a 't' when it is in different places in a sentence. You will likely have many different variations. It is no simple thing to get all those angles correct in a sample. Try having someone write a sentence or two and see if you can copy their form exactly. Have them try to copy yours. It is no small feat.

A good forger will tell you that to write like someone else you truly need to become the writer, feel their way of feeling, think their way of thinking, use your hand and body as they use theirs. It is every bit as much a mind game as it is just writing.

Think like a Criminal to write like a Criminal. Think like a Saint to write like a Saint. It's up to you to choose how you write, what your writing says of you. Saints and Criminals all use the same letters and digits we do. They weren't born a Saint or a Criminal but somewhere along the path learned other ways of doing and being and so changed their destiny.

Had we been there along the way to see, as they lived their life and made their choices, no doubt their hand would have fluctuated and altered as they made their way. If we could have watched and listened, we would have glimpsed a life quietly telling its tales of the gifts and the secrets in yet another *hand behind the word.*

5

Cultural And Historical Perspectives in Handwriting

J ust to get used to looking at some variations in handwriting, let's look briefly at some examples of a few different cultures' different forms. First, an Englishwoman (albeit a very theatrical and expressive one, hence the oversized script) whose quick literary mind and dry sense of humor show up in this form of English writing. She says that she has Americanized her digits, especially the 1 and 7 which otherwise would have looked more like this next sample.

On the next page, a smaller English hand, this one male. Although it is clearly quite different, still it has that playfulness, humor, quick mind. This writer is not as theatrical as the woman above. With the order and upright lean to the hand we can see that he is more reserved, but far from quiet. Note the form of the digits and the basic "feel" of the hand. Can you feel the similarities of the two?

1 2 3 4 5 6 7 8 9 0
1 2 3 4 5 6 7 8 1 0
1 2 3 4 5 6 7 8 1 0
1 2 3 4 5 6 7 8 9 0.

for you in researching you book.
14 August 1991.

Though both of these writers well engage and intensely link with their correspondents and conversants, there is in each hand a kind of distance and reservation. See the separation of the digits, even in the date? These are cues of reserve and distance.

Primary school origins affect how we make our digits and basic strokes for life. That is one reason there is such continuity in form across a culture. Most children go through the same training and tend to come out with digits relatively more similar to the rest of the hand.

German

Let's look now at a couple of examples from native Germans. Comparing and contrasting them with the British ones, see what patterns you notice.

Structurally similar, these two are quite different from the English samples and at the same time, fairly different from each other. Scale is consistent between them, so you can tell there is a difference in the size of handwriting. From that difference, might

1234567890

1234567890

1234567890

1234567890

Best wishes for your return to the States!

11/05/97

you guess which writer is an artist who likes to live larger than life and which is a quieter social scientist? Which one has an artistic / theatrical flair similar to the English woman above?

1 2 3 4 5 6 7 8 9 0

1 2 3 4 5 6 7 8 9 0

Formen mit unterfit Sehr empfehlens wel

28. April, 1997

Yes, it is the second sample who is the full-time artist; the first one is an anthropologist. He actually has quite a gentle and creative artistic side, too, as we see in some of his strokes. But his is more matter of fact and less flamboyant than the artist's playful (and sometimes harsh) oversized writing.

French

Next, a couple of French samples. Do you notice that the form is unique and yet it does have elements similar to both the German and the English samples above? The writer on the right, below, has Americanized his 7 and 9, though for some reason not the 1.

The familiar up-swoop 1 found in both these hands is very characteristic of a French hand. It is a sign of diplomacy and aloofness. Can you tell that this first French writer is more talkative and outgoing (lots of loops and full middle zone, a playful engaging 2, 5, 8, 9; rather large hand) whereas the neat and tidy writer on the right is more a scientist?

Notice his margins, on the digits, too. Do you remember what that would mean?

He tends to be always running headlong into the future. Early adopter, prefers promises of tomorrow rather than thinking about the past.

And that fits; he is a math and sciences student who has always been very interested in being one of the first in line to try out new mechanical or electronic toys. He has many of them! He is also a philosopher as his other main interest. Can you see how the stems of his letters are tall and reaching up? That fits, too.

Italian

Next, a rather French-looking hand. This writer is actually Italian by birth, but his numbers don't much look like it. He is an artistic visionary thinker, with some French traits and loves both languages, traveling extensively.

1234567890
1234567890
1234567890
1234567890

Un incontro interessante
in viaggio da Milano e
Bologna — 25/3/93

He has a softer, quieter hand than many Italians, paralleling his quiet gentle personality. His fascination with language, comparative religion and art show in the height and gentle curves of the numbers. Notice especially the 1's, 2's, 4's.

12345

Then look at the next two samples. These two are both Italians, too, but quite different from the one above. One of them is a female, one a male. See if you can figure out which one is which. One is a friendly, talkative middle-aged woman, opinionated and a bit given to depression. The other, her neighbor, is a smiling and soft-spoken young priest of about thirty-five. Which do you suppose is which?

If you speak Italian then the answer is obvious because of what the priest wrote. But of course since you are being that true analyst who completely ignores content and just looks at form (!) then you should be able to guess which writer seems more quiet.

1234567890
1234567890
1234567890
1234567890

È stata una bellissima serata grazie della compagnia ciao

08 - 05 - 97

One advantage of learning from foreign language samples is that you may be less inclined to read it for content. Perhaps that way you will better be able to see the sample as just shapes and patterns on a page. That's useful. Look at how the words cluster or distribute across the page, how the overall line is even or not. See how it feels. Which one feels quietest? Which feels most talkative? What does a talkative hand look like in English? You have probably seen hundreds of them. That should give you a clue.

In order to get an emotional picture of the hand behind the word, imagine what it would feel like to write like either or both of them. It requires more than just your reader's brain to do this. You will need to practically breathe yourself into the hand.

Or, if you wish, take out a piece of paper and try to write each of them. Try to feel which one is quieter.

1 2 3 4 5 6 7 8 9 0
1 2 3 4 5 6 7 8 9 0
1 2 3 4 5 6 7 8 9 0
1 2 3 4 5 6 7 8 9 0
1 2 3 4 5 6 7 8 9 0

Se dovessi camminare in una
valle oscura, non temo nulla,
perché tu Signore, sei con me.

So, have you made your decision? Can you tell which is the priest's and which is his talkative neighbor? Which is more contemplative, less given to having loud opinions? As you may have by now guessed, the second sample here is the priest. He's writing from the Lord's Prayer.

His talkative neighbor lady is on the facing page. Notice the way her baseline slopes downward. That's her depression. The largeness and loops, that's her talkativeness.

Her 7 also has the gossip's characteristic looped opinionation tic in it very prominently at the top left. Notice how quiet the priest's 7 (and his fellow Italian on the previous page) is by comparison. Very different.

Thai

Finally on the cultural perspectives, let's look at some Thai writing. What might we expect Thai handwriting to say about its people?

1 2 3 4 5 6 7 8 9 0
1 2 3 4 5 6 7 8 9 0
1 2 3 4 5 6 7 8 9 0
1 2 3 4 5 6 7 8 9 0

Tomorrow I will go back home.

คืนๆ: กลับบ้าน พรุ่งนี้ .

Aug 11 ,94

Perhaps friendly, smiling, respectful, self-contained? Thai handwriting is usually a very gentle hand, males and females alike. Notice that even in English, this writing is quite a bit smaller and neater than most Americans write. What does that say about us as a people? And what does it say about the Thai people?

With most Thai's writing rather small, perhaps that cultural trait has something to do with an intricate and delicate awareness of subtle power, a tendency to use space wisely, to mind the rules, to work well with others, to be dedicated to industrious pursuit of knowledge and accomplishments, though rather quietly so.

The American Hand

Certainly that doesn't sound too much like the typical American creed, does it? As a people and a culture, we aren't so quiet about our accomplishments, our ideals, our pursuits.

Neither do we write as intricately as the Thai. In fact, we tend to have such a bravado and intensity in our hand that when Americans write as small and neatly as Thai writing, they may generally find themselves judged for being picky, self-conscious, shy, introverted. Often as a rule, our cultural handwriting reflects more a boldness and brashness, a raw innovation and optimism, a fighting spirit for which Americans are often labeled overseas.

Speaking of overseas, as a research item it might be interesting sometime to take a look at the handwriting of world leaders when they come together for a summit meeting or a conference. Just like any other team of colleagues (and those at the helm of nations of the world would certainly be considered colleagues on the same team) a joint sample could say quite a bit about how they get along.

Historical Political Leaders

It is interesting to think about the way world politics might play out in handwriting. If we were to be able to see world leaders' handwriting on a regular basis we might have a better idea what's going on behind the scenes. We'd see machinations and power struggles, respects and resentments, alliances and fears.

We'd also likely see who tends to tell the truth and serve the best interests of the people and who repeatedly only prevaricates, equivocates and evades in a pompous self-serving charade. Those who ascend to power are often the ones most apt to want to use and abuse it. It is perhaps no surprise that leaders often have a strong hand, in more ways than one.

One interesting very doable thing about handwriting and politics is that we can go back in history and take a look at the handwriting of world leaders of the past. When we do, we can see something of their relationship to one another, who they are, how they behave and how they write.

Waterloo

Let's take a look at a short side-by-side clip of history from the early 1800's when a couple of Europeans got together .in a place called Waterloo to settle their differences. Neither Napoleon nor Lord Wellington had exactly lovely handwriting to look at but then that's not usually what a military leader needs most. One thing which stands out immediately about these two is their major differences.

Napoleon seems an optimistic dreamer, quiet and moody.

Lord Wellington, however, was strong and passionate and seemed to hold to the motto, *"Forward ever, backward never!"*

His hand suggests a great deal more confidence and pushiness than his opponent mustered. The two samples here are of the same scale, though currently only about one half of their real size. Napoleon's tiny, moody and flourished hand clearly seems no contest for Wellington's tall, firm brashness. It seems likely from the handwriting that Napoleon would have tended to rely more on deceit, trickery and pure guile whereas Wellington could have met all of that with some of his own and dished out a massive wallop as well.

If you're a history buff, you already know who won this battle. Napoleon may be on top here, but he didn't come out on top at Waterloo.

A handwriting analyst who didn't yet know but who was looking over the situation from qualities in each hand might guess something about how the two fought. Napoleon's smaller tightly held writing clashing with Wellington's loud brash forward push could probably make a point.

U.S. Civil War

Moving forward another fifty years or so, we come upon a couple of adversaries on the other side of the Atlantic, during the Civil War:

Looking at the full size signatures of these two strong and passionate opposing generals of the war, we see perhaps a part of the reason why the intense fighting went on so long. This was a very different set of opponents than Waterloo's Napoleon and Wellington. Both signatures suggest an imposing presence.

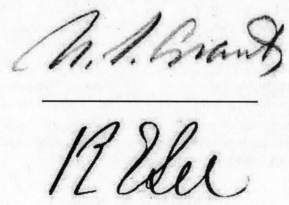

Lee and Grant were both great proud generals, trained superbly as cadets in West Point's Long Gray Line where they pledged fidelity to "Duty, Honor, Country." It was perhaps a great irony that Grant was not an outstanding cadet while at the Academy though Lee had finished second in his class. Lee had also been Superintendent at West Point only ten years before the war he opposed. Fifteen years Grant's senior, Lee surrendered at Appomattox on April 2nd 1865, just twenty-five days short of Grant's forty-third birthday.

Incidentally, a point you will see again later is well illustrated here: Pencils do not make good samples. Grant, especially after becoming President, had a preference for pencils for his informal writing. I used this pencil sample to illustrate why we prefer ink.

World War II: Europe

Moving forward another sixty-five years we arrive at the 1930's, where we find the world in a deep depression after the economic collapse of 1929. Situations are building to the brink of another tumultuous world war. At center stage of this inevitable war is an arrogant little brute of a man, a well-read Austrian-born high school dropout who emigrated from Austria to his father's homeland and got himself elected German Chancellor.

Having fought in World War I, he only advanced to the rank of corporal. But as Chancellor fifteen years later, Adolf Hitler seized command of the German army and changed the course of history. His tiny signature with bizarre narcissistic symbolism shows signs of a true megalomaniac. His first name disappears altogether but in its place, he represents himself with a lone lightning bolt. The last name has a ruthless rightward lean and disregards both baseline and spacing. It begins with an inflated and overindulgent "H" and then degrades into an indiscernible sideways downward scribble to the end. A truly bizarre signature.

World War II: America

For another set of samples from World War II, we go to the other side of the Atlantic and come to a couple of leaders who found themselves in a bit of an internal power struggle. You may recognize these two Americans. If you had to guess which one was a more fiery communicator, you might be right.

The sample on top is that of Harry Truman, who seems to have a little higher ideals and likes to talk about them. Notice how tall and thin his hand is. It also has many little waves in the middle zone with an upbeat tail at the end. These are signs that this is someone who likes to think and talk and work things through in a conversational straightforward style.

With his capital "T" he's apt to have a fiery temper and no patience with passive aggressive non-communicators who might try blocking him, shutting him down or taking him for granted. Ironically, though, that's exactly what history tells us happened between these two.

MacArthur never liked having Truman on top, so I put him on the bottom here just to remind him who's boss. MacArthur was another of the West Point generals, top in his class. He had his own views of how the world looked and, quite unlike Truman, did not always care to talk about it. The power and force of his hand is

from blunt vertical strokes with no middle zone presence at all. He tends to be much less sensitive and idealistic and even has a number of angular back-focused loops and hooks in his hand. These traits don't bode well for a willingness to communicate very openly with anyone, let alone someone calling himself the boss.

Historians will recall that the power struggle between President Harry Truman and General Douglas MacArthur culminated in April 1951 when the General was recalled from the field and fired for insubordination. As we might expect from the passive-aggressive yet self-underlined master that he saw himself, MacArthur returned home as requested, but made a bold show of doing so with the flourish of a hero's welcome just to prove who was pulling his strings. This no doubt infuriated the President who, as we might expect from his idealism and fire, would have been livid about what he probably regarded as a passive-aggressive spectacle.

America's First Female General

As long as we're on the subject of military leaders, let's include here the first female general in the history of the U. S. Army, Brigadier General Mary Clarke. Notice how she has a very balanced hand and makes full use of all three zones, the upper zone, middle zone and lower zone, suggesting that she is a very well-rounded and alert leader.

Capable of both clear headed thinking and sensitivity on the fly, she is certainly a strong leader, but very much more detached and matter-of-fact than the West Point generals of the Civil War whom we saw above.

Notice the interesting way General Clarke terminates her last name. The economy stroke of making a "k" and an "e" in such close succession gives her a kind of rebellious looking "e" at the end of her name.

This would suggest an ability to hold firm under pressure, yet a willingness to be confrontational where necessary. These were no doubt fitting qualities for a woman who probably had to deal with more than her share of challenge as the first woman in the Army to reach the rank of general.

A Literary Alliance

We see a similar rebellious "e" in Pauline Pfeiffer Hemingway's signature and her husband's as well, but less so. Like General Clarke, Pauline Pfeiffer Hemingway would have had some challenges to overcome, being the second of four wives of Ernest Hemingway.

Being married to such an enigmatic and moody man as Hemingway would have been quite a challenge in itself but she had other forces to deal with as well. Pauline's signature suggests she was no shrinking violet and so, no doubt, added quite some challenge of her own to the mix.

Looking at their signatures together, there is a coolness and distance in the relationship, in the way his hand stands almost vertical with an excessive focus on the ideal and theoretical upper zone whereas Pauline's is more naturally slanted to the right with a fuller presence in the here-and-now of the middle zone.

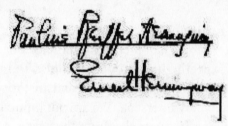

No doubt these two had quite significant arguments permeating the marriage with more than a few challenges to overcome. Pauline's industrious, challenging and rebellious "e" appears four times in her signature. She would certainly have been one to speak her mind and must have been quite a powerful force to reckon with not only as a partner but as a social mover and shaker, too.

Note the way she did not care to lean on the Hemingway name at all, but was perfectly comfortable just being a Pfeiffer. We can read "Pfeiffer" quite easily. It is actually the tallest part of her signature, a very significant statement about her sense of identity.

"Hemingway," on the other hand, seems little more than just a couple of slices and a few loops of boring necessity she dutifully carried out. She was not overly invested in taking on this name.

Setting a couple people's hands together and seeing how the interplay tells other stories can be a very useful way to get to know someone. Especially when two people come together and take the same name, it can be an interesting reflection on their feelings about it, whether it's a business name, a married name, or a work project's team name. How the two people write it is often very instructive about their feelings for the name and their shared experience.

This is just one of many small details we see in signatures which tell interesting stories about the writers. If, as in the case of many of these, we already know something of their history, then the handwriting can fill in some of the gaps we might not otherwise have known about. It is again a case of history speaking to us as though our writers were here with us today.

Why We Care

Understanding some of the cultural and historical perspective from which the writers come is sometimes useful for a handwriting analyst or researcher expecting to deal with samples from various cultures and ages. As you see, handwriting and history have no trouble interacting when they intersect. We are not limited by geography or time when we look into samples from the past.

Any sample we have of a writer, living or dead, from any culture will have messages from the time period and culture which reflect something of how people write, believe, behave and interact.

By far the most interesting aspect of studying history through handwriting is each writer's unique expression of personality and essence, history and experience interwoven right into the writing. This personal flavor makes for a truly delightful bonus in the course of the research as we occasionally get that secret glance into the hand behind the word.

Rebels and Leaders, Artists and Visionaries

There will be rebels and leaders, artists and visionaries in all cultures who will push whatever limits they are given and will see the world their own way. And on the other end of the spectrum, great masses of conformists and followers, those necessary worker bees and drones so important for the success of a society. One thing which stands out (or perhaps doesn't stand out) about the handwriting of the middle ground conformist is how typically it conforms and fits into the grey cultural perspective and norm from which it originated.

But not so with rebels and leaders, visionaries and artists. We find that they are rarely satisfied to fit into whatever box of conformity they are offered, each for their own reason. They often give us something totally different to consider for boundaries, though not necessarily in any way we'd expect.

The Rebel Without A Cause

No doubt James Dean was one of those artists and rebels, but his signature two months before his death suggests that at twenty-four he wasn't near the rebel inside that he liked to play outside.

Rather, we see a quiet reserved demeanor who could probably cry very easily, a sensitive nature and strong business head about him. Certainly he isn't exactly the *Rebel Without a Cause* he so well portrayed. But then, he always was a pretty good actor!

Dreamers and visionaries, actors and artists will usually show us something of their dissatisfaction with conformity in their handwriting.

Sometimes they pull back against one line, sometimes they push forward against another. Sometimes for a signature they disregard lines altogether and will redefine the page or practically slash it angrily apart with deep cutting strokes as if to say, "I cut ties to anything not me!"

Or they may quickly and expertly embellish a page every time with intricacies of a unique signature like piano virtuoso Wladziu Liberace, whose trademark flourish autograph probably serves to remind most of us how very plain and simple we are. The ornate audacity of a signature like his makes us smile, asks new questions, inspires new steps out in our blue suede shoes. One thing it surely asks is why we settle, why we argue for our limitations, why we allow ourselves to be defined and confined between the lines of the simple and the regular. Isn't life more interesting than that?

Certainly a signature like Liberace's is unique and different, rare and extraordinary. And for how it's seen in handwriting analysis, it's fine. In fact, it's great.

Personality in a Signature

Personality in handwriting is a good thing, especially in the signature. It tells us more about the way the writer chooses to be presented, play by the rules or break them, communicate in a flamboyant expressive style or quietly blend in with the grey conformity of the masses.

Of course, we wouldn't want to see someone drawing pictures in every phrase he writes, but a signature is a special place in the hand. It's the place you get to play, get to define how you want the world to see you, what goals and ambitions you set for yourself. The signature is a special window into the soul of the writer; it is the "I's" of handwriting.

Handwriting is a function not only of these various levels of the "I's" of who we are, but also of the cultural and historical perspective from which we came.

A part of the foundation of our writing is laid down for us in fourth grade penmanship class; another part is chipped and whittled as we make our way in the trials and traumas of experience; yet another part of the handwriting is from our body, its health and makeup. But by far the most interesting and most flexible part of our handwriting is the creative essence we spill into it every time we joyfully choose another way to write.

Too many of us forget that handwriting is creativity and opportunity. It is both the story teller and the story. It is a radiant jewel in the collective treasure of who we are. We do well to take good care of it, tend it, play with it, embrace it and learn from it. It is a wonderful multi-layered reflection of who we are.

Handwriting and its story are a participative study. You will learn best by planning to collect a few samples while you read and study material here. Take the time to write samples of your own, too. Writing a complete sample in your book every few days while you study will give you a re-traceable path, a record of who and where you were emotionally, intellectually and spiritually as you made your way along this path of study.

It is entirely possible that you will learn and grow and change a bit over the course of your handwriting studies. Having a handwritten record of that process could be an invaluable gift for you or your biographers to be able to tip-toe through your life with these handwritten love notes from you. Or if that seems too personal and invasive, then you can always instruct your heirs to burn your sample books. But I hope you'll at least consider writing the samples first anyway. There are some blank sample forms in Appendix I at the back of this book where you can write several samples as you go.

Take a risk to take a look into the fascinating being you are. You will find that the more samples you take of your own writing, the more you'll discover about your own personal historical and cultural perspective. You are history, you are culture and you are the very essence of a *hand behind the word.*

6

The JAQS Sample Format
The Digits in Handwriting, Too

Handwriting is a personalized reflection of a system we once used on a daily basis to record life around us. With the advent of computers, cell phones and other personal information managers, communication has been moving to forms other than handwriting. Many writers these days are using handwriting only very rarely for more than a line or two of notes.

But most everyone everyday writes at least a few numbers, their name, signature, the date and a little text. These are the very five elements we use for the *JAQS Style* sample format.

You'll notice that many of the samples you have seen so far have included a series of digits with the text. That's because these are samples from the *JAQS Style* sample format. It is a sample format from which *Just A Quick Sample* offers to provide you *Just A Quick Story* about the writer before you.

The *JAQS Style* format is very different from what many handwriting analysts will be accustomed to using. It starts by taking an unlined white page and folding it in half both directions to form a quarter sheet size. Then we ask the writer to choose a comfortable ink pen (not felt tip, permanent marker or pencil) and on one of the quarter panels, write four rows of digits, a signature, printed name, paragraph of choice to fill out the rest of the page, and the date. That's it. Quite a small sample but a very useful one. There are some blank *JAQS Style* sample sheets in the back of this book for actually taking your first samples.

Some handwriting analysts may be surprised to see a sample so short and may wonder how useful it can be in providing the information they are accustomed to collecting in much longer form. But when a brief sample includes at least the minimum requirements as outlined, its brevity is perhaps one of the *JAQS* format's finest assets.

The *JAQS Style* sample is flexible enough to suit most requirements and is ideal as a standardized research tool. It can provide a rich and comparative data study in a plentiful format for basic analysis. For an analyst who understands the data, a fuller sample is usually not necessary. If you're thinking there is not much variety in the digits, think again. Here are a few we'll review:

	A	B	C	D	E	F	G	H	J	K
1	1	1	1	1	1	1	1	1	1	1
2	2	2	2	2	2	2	2	2	2	2
3	3	3	3	3	3	3	3	3	3	3
4	4	4	4	4	4	4	4	4	4	4
5	5	5	5	5	5	5	5	5	5	5
6	6	6	6	6	6	6	6	6	6	6
7	7	7	7	7	7	7	7	7	7	7
8	8	8	8	8	8	8	8	8	8	8
9	9	9	9	9	9	9	9	9	9	9
0	0	0	0	0	0	0	0	0	0	0

A Brief Legend of the Digits in the *JAQS Style* format

1	Sense of Self - who am I, how do I relate to others, am I comfortable being who I am?
2	Impersonal View of Other People - how I relate to and see the nameless people who serve me or interact with me daily.
3	Self and Others, Work and Neighbor Relations - how I relate to those named people at work, at home, in extended family, the neighborhood, etc.
4	More Intimate Relations, Sexuality and Relationship - how I see and participate in my most intimate relationships.
5	Spontaneity, Humor and the Way I Deal with Time - how I deal with planning, my sense of humor and my tendency to procrastinate all show up here.
6	Minor Irritations / Traumas - how I deal with the minor irritations of life including slights and prods or annoyances at work or at home; drivers who cut me off.
7	Sense of Principles - my ethical and decision-making foundations and view of the world which help me to navigate choice and ethics, resisting peer pressure, manipulations.
8	Major Traumas of Life - how I deal with life's major hits such as illness, loss, dislocation, abuse, abandonment, death, etc.
9	Sense of the Self and the World - how I see my reputation, my calling, vocation, job status, roles and needs at work.
0	The World - my view of history, politics, big picture ideas, culture, community and feelings of my place in it.

Acclimating to the *JAQS Style* Sample

One immediate difference people will notice about the *JAQS* format is the way it constricts space, having the sample page folded into a quarter sheet. Some analysts accustomed to a larger format will question the effect of restricting and constricting space like this and will wonder if and how this may affect the result. It does affect the resulting sample. This is both intentional and useful for the purpose of interpretation. In so doing, it helps to exaggerate certain emotional and interpersonal traits and expressions.

Many writers will simply go with the flow and not comment about the size at all. Writers who find themselves constricted and limited by the size will have already made a statement quite relevant to their personality: they require more space in order to feel comfortable, usually both figuratively and literally, too.

Conversely, there are some writers who immediately curl up happily in the comfort of this tiny little haven and say they feel much less anxiety with a small sheet than they do with the gaping void of a large blank page. So they are very happy to have a smaller sample size to work with. This, too, is a valid and relevant statement about such a personality. A more conventional sample may have taken much more space and time to make either point.

The other most noticeable difference between the *JAQS Style* sample and a more conventional one is those digits across the top of the page. Most analysts never specifically request or pay any attention to digits in handwriting at all. They will have little or no basis for understanding what may be hidden there.

In the *JAQS Style* sample there are four rows of digits for two primary reasons. First, so that we have enough digits there to be able to have a more genuine set in the event that an individual one or two here or there might seem out of form or misshapen. Secondly, many people will try and start out giving you digits the way they think they were supposed to write them from some theoretical right or wrong format quiz. But luckily most will actually tire of trying to be perfect by about row two or three so they will usually provide at least one or two genuine rows.

Digits are very useful in that they represent an orderly microcosm of all the basic stroke elements of handwriting in a tight and repetitive package which most everyone writes every day. Although digits do not typically reach extensively into the lower zone, they do offer interpretive parallels to inform the data there.

An Introduction to Single JAQS Digit Analysis

Before we go in depth about each of the digits individually, here are a series of number fragments taken from a few random *JAQS Style* samples. Rather than just giving you one digit out of context, there are three in a row so that you can get a feel for spacing and placement as well as form. See what you can guess for each of these.

Whether you realize it or not, you probably already have a feel for what's in some of these. Even if you don't think you know yet, try to take a guess. Answers will follow and be explained after this group of exercises.

Which one of these 678's seems more angry, willing to argue? Which might fly off the handle more quickly? Which one seems more dependable, although a bit controlling and stubborn?

And now these 567's: Which one probably has a nice smile and looks quite friendly, (the 5) yet tends to be passive-aggressive? (The 6)

Hint: look at the tail of the 6. Both of these are a little argumentative with tails like they have. But which one seems more apt to slink out of nowhere and pounce on you?

Which of these 345's is less friendly, less talkative? (Keeps a distance). Which is louder and has a more playful sense of humor? (Little smile in a rocker base). Which one idealizes relationship? (4).

Hint: Too much space between numbers is like standing too far away as you talk. Less friendly, less talkative. Playfulness in humor often has full rocker base in the 5. For relationship, we look at the 4. Which has a swooping idealized cross bar? Anywhere we see the idealized swoop (shown below: mainly in 2 or 4, but can also be in the top of a 3 or 7) it means this is a dreamy idealist.

Now the 890's: Which one of these was probably not feeling well when the sample was taken and may have been a hypochondriac as a child? (See the shape of the 8's, kind of like a 6 with a humpback on it). Which sees trauma or illness as a weakness? (The 8's again, pushes forward at all costs, tends to limit the size of how much of a trauma or illness it's willing to allow into the lower loop, which is the active part of life).

One of these 8's seems to feel like it's pouting and sad and the other is aloof and distant. Which is which? (Pouting will be full, round and watery. Aloof is sharper, distant, spaced out).

One 9 mixes business and friendship; the other is mistrustful, almost paranoid of business associates. Can you tell which is which? One of them seems to have something deceptive going on at work and seems a bit fearful of others watching over its world. Which is that? Overall which of these feels more comfortable, appealing or familiar to you? Why?

Answers

The 678's: The lower one seems more angry because it's out of sync with itself. Look at the way that 7 leans over too far to the right. And the 8 is opened up at the top, meaning that it isn't quite sure why it feels what it feels.

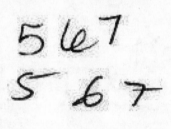

The lower one could probably fly off the handle sooner, because of the tiny loop in the 6 and the excessive lean of the 7. The top one is more of a pressure cooker, (larger controlled lower loop in the 6). Dependable (7) but double snowball / spotlight circles of the 8 says: rather controlling.

The 567's: The more passive-aggressive one is the one on the top. Look at the stress bow in the top of the 5. With the full formed smiling lower part of the 5, she's sweet, pleasant, kind. But look out when she blows!

With that razor sharp 7 and compressed loop in the 6, she means business and is apt to make things difficult for you if she doesn't get her way! Her 5 may say sweetness and smiles but the tail on that 6 can strike out and come after you! Both of these have a tail coming through the 6. We call that the arguing cat's tongue. But the one on top looks like it's ready to pounce and bite!

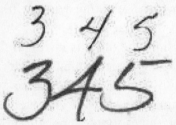

The 345's: The top one is less talkative. Notice the way the numbers are a bit too far separated from each other. There's a caution about relating to others very quickly.

The lower one tends to slide on in there, push everything together and chat up anyone and everyone! The playful sense of humor?

That's the lower one again. That full rocker base on the bottom of the 5 tells us that; it has a nice smile in it. The top 5's base is not even finished.

Who probably idealizes relationship? Top one. See that swooping horizontal cross stroke in the middle of the 4? That's a sign of the dreamy ideal. But notice that the horizontal stroke stopping at the main stem. The cross bar of a 4 is the relationship itself. This one means she's probably not in a relationship, or if she is, then she's stuck, not having any "fun."

The lower 4 has a very picky view of relationship (note the closed triangle) but a willingness to go for it if Perfection comes along (cross-bar goes through the stem). He also has what we call the stress foot, (a bending of the foot of the stem of a 1, 4, 7, 9) in this case, stress of self-concept / performance issue there.

890's: As to the hypochondriac: that's the top one. There's a noticeable sinister lean (backward) to both the 8 and the 9 here (an inward past focus sigh). The 8 also has a triangular compression of the oversized and pouting loops. Not quite a natural flow there. Probably wasn't feeling well that day and had some pressures of past business.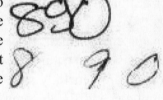

Which one tends to see trauma as a weakness? The lower one. Notice how tiny her 8's lower loop is. Hardly exists at all. The upper part of an 8 is our perception of trauma in life and the lower part of the 8 is how we incorporate that trauma back into our life view. In this case, it's hardly incorporated at all. She probably sees it as a weakness and not something to embrace or learn from, in stark contrast to the upper sample.

Neither one of these would be an ideal 8; ideally we'd have some kind of balance between the two, without over-exerting pressure or going to that snowball intense 8 which over analyzes and criticizes all.

Which of the 890's seems sad and pouty? That's the top one. The roundness and curling into itself is kind of like a pouting child. The top one is also the one which would probably mix business and friendship, too. Why? Because of that 9 tail and the way it wraps under itself like a 'g' and in this case leans over into the 0. All run together like that usually means mixes social roles; might tend to crash typical social role boundaries and blend between them. Work relations (getting along) is seen also in a 3. But the 9 (role as self in the world) deals with professional capacity, or role and reputation at work.

The colder starker sample on the bottom with all the digits so far apart seems a bit distant, cold, disinterested. In fact, if you look at the way the 9 is set off by itself and has that extra little double tic on the staff at its center, that's a strange manifestation about business and the world and tends to be a mark of mistrust and fear of business associates. There's probably a reason; it could point to some fear or dishonesty at work or some other work problems there.

We don't in general like to see overstrikes or doubly-formed characters like that. Hooks, overstrikes and smudges (as well as excessive intersecting lines and misshapen characters like this) in a hand are generally signs of deception and evasive thoughts or emotions and should send up a little flag to watch out for other signs of dishonesty and guile in this hand. I only gave you three digits of this writer, but you'll notice that none of the three could be considered exactly culturally standard. That is not an insignificant observation about a hand.

More Handwriting Basics

Learning handwriting analysis is a lot like learning to speak a foreign language. It's important to pay attention to as many of the nuts and bolts as possible and hopefully have some kind of idea about how they fit together. But there's no substitute for being willing to at some point just jump in and start using as much as you can. Sure, you'll make mistakes. And for a while the people you try communicating with will have no idea what you are saying.

But you were misunderstood and made mistakes the first time you studied a new language, too, when you were just a toddler. Do you remember how motivated and determined you were to jump in and keep trying? You really wanted to learn to communicate. I hope your motivation and determination can help you this time, too. You need to jump right in and take some samples from people around you so that you can start seeing some traits up close, start making some mistakes, then make sense of some nuts and bolts.

As you recall from Chapter Three we first look at the *gestalt* of a hand to get a feel for it. Then we can start zeroing in on what stands out about the hand. Then we look at the pieces and see what it's made of. It's important to get these in the right order and not start out looking at the pieces.

Like a foreign language, if you focus on trying to get all the pieces correct before you open your mouth, the conversation is going to be gone and you'll be sitting there alone and silent with no one even knowing you had something to say, let alone what it was. Take the risk to open up and begin the conversation. One of the things you will learn is that other people's curiosity and interest will help motivate you to learn, too.

Let's assume you understand that order, so you are aware that what I'm about to say is Step Three, looking at the detail, for any hand you are reviewing. Each digit by itself has a particular meaning. The digit needs to be seen in the context of the whole, but has its own unique piece of the puzzle to add as well.

Let's take a look now at the ten digits and some examples of what each of them can mean as we find them in a hand.

Digit By Digit Overview

1: Sense of Self

A	B	C	D	E	F	G	H	J	K
/	/	/	/	/	/	/	,	)	/

A Normal, plain, direct, confident.
B Discerning, aloof, picky, judgmental, cautious.
C Ambitious, practical, determined, stubborn.
D Diplomatic, artful, can be deceitful if signs show up somewhere else in the hand.
E Picky, judgmental, lower sense of self than B. (Shorter in size, but with larger tic at top than B, almost looks like a 7).
F Bent right: Worrier, stresses about health issues.
G Loop foot: Proud, vain, deceitful, pretentious.
H Low self esteem, depressed, fearful. (Tiny size).
J Bent left. Dishonest, seems guilty about something.
K Horizontal tic: Cold, mechanical, hesitant, quiet.

When you're looking through these digit example pages to find your own, yours may be a combination of two or more. If so, read all that apply. These only brush the surface of the variety of digit forms out there, but at least you'll get a better idea.

2: Impersonal Sense of Others

(How we see and interact with the people in our lives whose names we do not know and whom we may or may not see again: grocery clerks, people on the street, etc.).

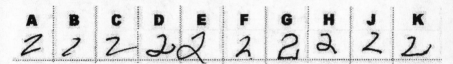

A Cautiously aloof, overworked, too busy, doesn't have time to listen well, but would like to try, stressed.

B Doesn't listen at all and doesn't want to. Aloof loner, can tend to be anti-social or lazy. May have trouble telling the truth.

C Involved with everyone, though only surface, official go-to person with all the answers, can have trouble connecting with people in meaningful ways because of time constraints.

D The truck-stop waitress 2! Great smile, can feign interest in anyone or anything. Genuinely happy and present. Knows how to listen very well.

E Tries to listen, though probably butts in too much. Is genuinely interested in other people's lives. Lives vicariously. Worries.

F Tries to listen to people, but has little patience with incompetence. Short temper, often cynical outlook.

G Cool detached mechanical listener. Will listen to anyone and offer advice to all. Always knows best.

H Cares about people but unsure how to relate. Cautious, prefers to err towards mistrust. Can be gullible.

J Caring listener but aloof. Can relate to most anyone.

K Playful almost childish communicator. Silly, fun.

3: Friend, Work and Neighbor Relations

(How we see and interact with people in our lives whose names we know; those familiar: friends, roommates, neighbors).

A	B	C	D	E	F	G	H	J	K
3	3	3	3	3	3	3	3	3	3

A   A bit of a loner. Unusually creative thinker, though impatient, can have a chip on the shoulder. Lacks confidence to succeed.

B   Good worker, but somewhat an elitist. Good leader.

C   Usually is popular, but isn't always the brightest bulb in the string. Tries hard and means well, so be nice!

D   Good worker. Picky and sometimes intolerant. Detail oriented, perhaps a bit too much so.

E   Good worker, pleasant to work with. Can sometimes be a little too bossy. Full of self and stories. Friendly, loves to talk.

F   A dreamy distant cousin to aloof. Gets lost a lot, forgets to listen, has to do things two or three times. May be an Aquarius!

G   Picky, judgmental, overbearing but unfortunately is also usually right. Tough partner, but a good teacher.

H   Flamboyant dreamy idealist. Judgmental. Good worker, popular, but can't stand to get shoes dirty in the process!

J   Good worker especially if it was their idea. Motherly, kind, tend to obsess a bit about repeating too many directions.

K   Feels like an in-law. Never quite fits in. Tries hard, but never seems to be able to feel appreciated. Knows how to go through all the right motions. Determined. Distant.

4: Sexuality and Intimate Relationships

(How we feel about ourselves and get along in our most intimate relationships. How we're apt to treat a partner in a relationship).

A	B	C	D	E	F	G	H	J	K
4	4	4	4	4	4	4	4	4	4

A The librarian's 4. Picky, idealistic, romantic. Slow to start, hard to catch, but well worth it if you have the stamina to try.

B Loves to read romance novels in secret and dream about what love would be like. Prefers reading.

C Open-minded, but tends to be a little slow. Can be frustrated by relationship. Sighs a lot, tries a lot, maybe even cries a lot.

D Pushy and self-impressed about being a good partner. Can sell anything, but forgets that love isn't salesmanship! May treat people like playthings with pet names. Plays around at work.

E Interesting. Creative. Can suggest things like making love swinging from a tree. Tends to be fun but quite eccentric.

F Scientific, theoretical mechanical. Has to test everything before beginning. Enough planning. Lets just get on with it!

G "Oops. Of course you mean the world to me, Honey. Sorry. Does it count if I just thought it?" Missing a values perspective in relationship. Takes partner for granted; relationship and partner are indiscernible from one another.

H A little bit shy and lacking in confidence in love. Knows to please partner first, but hesitates about making any moves.

J Driven to make relationship work. Satisfies partner first (secondary stem tallest). Selfless, joyful and sensual.

K Oh, so you tend to believe the world revolves around you about 4-6 days a week and the other days are when you're resting? Hmmm... And your partner keeps you?

5: Spontaneity, Humor, Time & Planning

(The sense of humor, ability to show up on time, appreciation for planning and keeping things well arranged in time order).

A Has to pre-tell and re-tell the punch line to make sure you get it. So perfect, should be a wedding planner.

B Dedicated, good natured, sometimes boring but dependable as a good friend to go out with.

C Busy worker. No time for humor. Always thinking about the next deal. So much so, misses lunch.

D Plans way ahead for every possible problem but missed the bus while planning the route. Didn't notice yet.

E Jolly, playful, talkative. Can sometimes miss a train, but has fun using that time in other creative ways.

F Spins wheels and thinks a lot; may need help slowing down. Always moving: needs to be shackled to the desk to be found.

G Stressed out about time and plans. Would love to laugh if it's in the budget this month. It's not.

H Depressed about tomorrow's plan. Needs a good kick or distraction if you have one handy. Worries too much.

J Can provide a few too many distractions. Forgets to go to work on time. Too busy having fun to bother with duties.

K Diligent 9-5'er. Plays by the rules and keeps time cards accurate to the second. Studies the weather.

6: Dealing With the Minor Irritations of Life

(What happens when someone asks us to work late; cuts us off in traffic; puts us on hold a few too many times).

A Passive, will tolerate quite a bit before blowing. Good colleague as long as you're not debaters. You'd lose.

B The micro-manager is in. Please bring your problems to the front of the room and take a number publicly.

C "Do I look like I care?" Up tight and no time for problems. Doesn't deal well with irritations, large or small. Stressed.

D Notice the beady eye peering into you. Watches things like a hawk. Can tell you moved those three paperclips 4" to the left!

E Takes on too much responsibility whether asked to or not. Wouldn't be happy if they weren't miserable. Can be overweight.

F This person is ready to cry over milk spilled from 12 years ago. Can't get over slights or grudges. Difficult trusting / forgiving.

G Notice the cat's tongue lashing through the loop? You're about to be chastised, argued with or put in your place. Be forewarned.

H "Yes, Sweetie, thanks for trying to help. But next time, just mind your own business. I got it covered." Can be a little bossy and territorial. (Swooped main stem, small loop).

J Still trying to figure out if that was annoying or a manifestation on a theoretical disturbance continuum. Thinks too much!

K Seeks to lasso you into an argument if you get close enough. You know you're guilty, no point in arguing. (lasso stem loop).

7: Sense of Principles

(Big Picture views of principles; susceptibility to peer pressure; ability to make own decisions and stay clear about boundaries).

A	B	C	D	E	F	G	H	J	K
7	7	7	7	7	7	7	7	7	7

A 7's cross-bar can be there or not. If it's there, we look to see if it's high or low or right or left. But they are neither good nor bad and are not relevant parts of this interpretation. This illustrates basic structure and form only, not the presence or absence of a cross-bar.

A Always willing to help you learn to live by their principles du jour. Can't be bothered to do it themselves (tic but loose corner).

B Sharp mind, sharp tongue. Sharper knife. Probably not the best place to pick a fight. Not much patience.

C Thinker and theorist. Willing to let you know what they think, why, and how often. They love to argue.

D Can drone on for hours about ethics and theory and utopian principles in 19th century literature.

E Diplomatic and willing to invent new principles if they would go better with what you're having for dinner.

F A little stressed about how to keep you on track of where you're supposed to be. Can't be bothered to tend their principles, however. Too busy with the world's.

G Says things like: "Oh, now, don't be such a spoil sport. It's only for tonight. Then I'll quit." Not always ethical. Playful.

H Doesn't even know what principles are. It's not a choice, it's just a lack of exposure. So we can't judge too harshly, eh?

J Would love to stand up for principles but is fearful of the responsibility. A bit naive and worried about the past. Stubborn.

K Very sharp and very bright. A forward mover and shaker.

8: Dealing With Life's Major Traumas

(This is where we store the Big Stuff... dealing with major illnesses, deaths in the family, loss of job or relationship, abuse and tragedy).

A Likes to measure and track everything, always. Anticipates the weather in advance. Sometimes paralyzed by inward focus.

B Charming control freak. (Angular double loop) Is usually right most of the time. Good under pressure.

C Future oriented, (tail) hopeful, good problem solver.

D Can get hit by a bus and not notice it. (Top wide open, but "in motion" opening) Not slowed by pessimists or fear, let alone tire tracks on the back.

E Meticulously controlling (perfection of form). Practically requires pre-authorization for a sneeze or a coffee break. Wow.

F Ultra aware of everything wrong in the world (oversized upper loop); tends to be constipated. Needs to let go. Can be overly world focused, in a narcissistic and overbearing way.

G "Life is sometimes messy and trauma needs to be pondered. Don't bother me until I figure it all out." The thinker. Flat top.

H Tends to live in the past; looking for the past to solve the world's problems. "What's that? The past is gone? Oh, No!"

J (starts the 8 at the bottom left) Creative, unique thinker. Tends to see the world upside down. Falls over a lot as a result of not understanding gravity.

K Still controlling. So controlling they bumped off the competitor to show up twice in this list of ten eights! Sometimes shows up as double snowball 8's: two evenly stacked circles. The double spotlight or double snowball 8's usually mean fear of loss of power and control.

9: Sense of Self in the World / Self & the World

(Made up of a stem which represents the self and a circle which represents the world. Together: reputation, profession, calling).

A	B	C	D	E	F	G	H	J	K
9	9	9	9	9	9	4	9	9	9

A Strong, good worker, a little shy (short stem).

B Determined and strong worker. Independent but may be selfish. (Stem goes above loop).

C A bit too talkative, (large foot loop) although the entire world seems related in this person's view of things.

D Another all-the-world-is-linked view, but this one has less need to chatter and be noticed. Better slant, too.

E A little too concerned about image. (Center isn't closed). Academically seems to know the big picture, but theory doesn't always match experience.

F Can be mechanical and a bit harsh about world view. (Lower loop is almost square at stem).

G Has little faith in others (open top) but doesn't believe in self much either. (Short stem).

H Can get a little antagonistic at work from memories of teen abuse. (Sinister hook) Feels a need to talk it out.

J Work now is stressful. (Bent stress foot at bottom). Nose to the grindstone helps, but when will it end? (Tight).

K Worries about place in the world. (Loop separated from stem) Sighs a lot, trying to work hard between bouts of self-doubt and self-pity. (Foot tic).

0: Sense of the World, History and Larger Community

(How we fit into and see our world. How we are affected by the big picture of history, politics, community and everything around us).

A	B	C	D	E	F	G	H	J	K

A A little too busy with living in tomorrow. Loves to plan and look forward. Busy little bee leaning way far forward.

B Feels flattened by the pressures of world's burden.

C Scientific or computer background; trying too hard to always be right. (Slash).

D Revisionist about the past. Makes up stories to pull heart-strings or open doors. (Tangle lower left close).

E "The world is a tough, lonely 'medication-required' place." Possibly addicted to drugs, alcohol or drama. (Stabbed heart).

F "Isn't the world a lovely place!? All is normal and healthy, happy, whole." Good form; a sigh of satisfaction. "Ahh!"

G "All is well for the most part; I might have to worry a bit about yesterday, but later." (Slight tic upper left).

H "Yesterday was a fast life, but I got away with it. Try not to remind me." (Open tail, upper left).

J "Tomorrow may be a fast life. I'll try to get away with it!" (Open tail upper right).

K "What is the meaning of Life? Is there a God? Why do I feel so forsaken?" Dramatically philosophical; feelings of disconnection from Spirit and things holy. (Open top).

Applying Your Knowledge on a Broader Basis

As you will recall, not many of the sample images in the book would be considered normal traits you would be apt to see every day in your own handwriting or someone else's. It has taken thousands of samples collected to get some of these. But one way to help spice up a sample collection is to try and get samples from the stranger people in your life, too. That's stranger as in strange.

Think about who might be able to give you some insight into some exaggerated forms. Get a sample from people who might seem more outgoing than the average or more odd than the average or more artistic, mechanical or even more angry than the average (if you can get close enough to get a sample!)

You probably already know your friends and family well enough to know who might fit the bill for having some of these exaggerated traits. They're the ones who will be able to give you some of your best first samples.

As you broaden and deepen your studies, you'll continue to be pleased with yourself when you understand a pattern in one set of data and are able to apply it to new samples. Find one thing that makes sense to you now and go with it until you get it down. Study only angles on 7's, rocker bases on 3's, cross bars on 4's, etc.

Symbology of the Torch

As you take samples and look at people's handwriting, talk to them about some of what you think it means. Ask for their immediate feedback as to whether or not you're on the right track. Most people will probably be interested and will tell the truth when you ask them to confirm what you see. Not everyone, but most. Some will not appreciate that you can see anything at all and so may deny it's there. But these are your teachers, too. When we're on a path of exploration from the darkness of curiosity to the light of understanding, everyone we meet along the path is one of our teachers.

As we pick up our skills, like torches, the better we apply them the better we see. Sometimes we learn by getting close to the fire so that we can see better. And sometimes we learn by stumbling into the fire to feel what it is like to get burned. Either way, we learn. Those of us who carry a torch are best advised to bear in mind it is the light we seek and not the heat.

Be thinking about this as you consider handwriting analysis. Think about the torch it represents and how you will bear that torch. In general, what is handwriting analysis? It is a call to observe details, then translate and relate them to meaning and interpretation, then reflect and selectively share what you see.

Like a torch, handwriting analysis can enlighten or burn the observer or the observed. If you reach for it too fast, or try to pass it off without making sure you have connected with the recipient you're apt to burn or get burned. You must also remember that the light does not come from you. You see it; you carry it; you share it. But you do not create it.

Best perhaps if we are able to see our observed writer and sample as the jewel they are, multifaceted, brilliantly beaming life's colorful essence in the hues of the handwriting. A jewel in the darkness can be misunderstood, as cold and hard and useless. But bring a torch near and it sings of color, dancing light and clarity we had not begun to imagine was even there until the light was cast upon it.

Seeing the Patterns

The more people you speak with about handwriting the more you will begin to notice patterns in your life. Take samples of people at home, at school, at work, in your house of worship, in your extended family, from friends and neighbors. Some of the patterns you will see will be subtle and others will be obvious.

As you look at your family's handwriting you may find that you all have the same back-slanted hand or you all write your last name the same strange way. Or perhaps several of you make 8's and 7's the same way. These are patterns. You may discover half the people at your work have bubbly writing, or most of the bosses print in CAPs, or all of your siblings have threaded signatures similar to yours.

Because of the choices we make in business or family or relationship interests, there will occur a series of lessons and challenges. We will repeat our methods of getting along or not, of solving problems or causing them in different places in our lives until we begin to deal with our life's particular lessons, learn from them and adapt to them.

If we are learning and growing, our handwriting is probably changing. All along, our handwriting (and the handwriting of those around us) is recording all of the behavioral tendencies of our lives in real time. It reflects our getting along or not, having a commitment to learn or perhaps having a fear of growing beyond our comfortable familiar bounds.

There is an infinitely rich resource there in the handwriting if we are willing to peek inside, dig around a bit, come back up to the surface with one of those glistening jewels of understanding.

Whenever we consciously or subconsciously choose an action or behavior in life, there is always someone who shows up with "the other half of our velcro" to drive us nuts, challenge us, complement us, or maybe even make us fall in love. It's a part of the dance of life. The dance card of that story is in your hand.

When we look at our handwriting and the handwriting of those around us, we will recognize some of our partners. We often find parallels there: shared handwriting patterns or complementary mirror image traits or reasons why we fit so well together, for better or for worse.

Take those samples! You will find handwriting you adore and handwriting you can hardly stand to look at. But it may not show up where you expect. Not all of our chosen beloved people will have handwriting we like. Sometimes it's our enemies' hand that will lure us in most effectively, for the lessons we will learn.

That is the beauty of this new dance number you have signed up for. It has some marvelous surprises in store for you as to who may be your next life teacher. I like to think that we're here on the planet to learn, grow and share. Perhaps it's not surprising that some of our teachers here will be our partners, co-workers, adversaries, parents or children. Life is full of teachers. Go out and get their handwriting!

Opening to Other Questions, Other Answers

Some of this may seem a little esoteric and "woo-woo" for some readers. You might wonder how relevant it is to handwriting to talk about "the other half of the velcro" or looking at life as a series of patterns or dances with our life's teachers.

You didn't sign up for a pop psychology course or a Zen workshop. You thought you came here to learn a few tidbits about the unsightly scrawl you see going across your desk every day and who these people are who wrote it. You've been wondering what else there might be to it, so you checked into a reference book.

Fair enough. This is a book about handwriting. But it is also more than that. It is an invitation to you to begin to look behind the scenes to a more personal view of *the hand behind the word* of who you are. Sometimes we need to tip-toe a bit into some of the darker corners of life's understanding where some of our early building blocks may have been mislaid. Instead of helping to build roads and bridges, we ended up turning them into high walls walling us in or walling us out. But it might be useful to know which.

This book is intentionally a very different view of handwriting, inviting you to think a bit about some aspects of your life you may not have considered lately. You are invited to take from it what you will. Come back again later for another read, another time to unwrap another layer of the onion. Keep unwrapping down to the heart and soul of understanding where you will meet a mirror image of yourself there carrying, like you, a torch of learning, growing and sharing. Your handwriting is that mirror.

Sample Books as Life Journals

Once you begin to formally collect and write samples, see them as a reference journal of your life. If you let them they are willing to serve as real and rich reflections from the contexts of your life. Let them remember for you. They have a date on them. They can hold stories if you let them.

Whenever you write a sample for yourself include something about the day you wrote it so that it serves as more than just a sample. Have others around you at the time write in the same sample book. It can keep an authentic record for you of who you were that day, encoded both as your message and your essence.

As you learn more about handwriting in years to come, you can come back and visit each day that you sampled and gaze into your life to be there again, just as we were with Abe Lincoln or Mother Theresa in Chapter Four. This is handwriting's gift. It continues to speak across miles and generations as an interesting and interested companion, working with us to help show us our life in the way of history and perspective, patterns and relationship.

Opening to Change

Sometimes we watch our handwriting scrawl out of us on a particular day and recognize that the handwriting reflects the life. We may make a conscious choice that day at that time to change that hand and the life behind it. The two are inexorably linked. We can't change our handwriting without changing our life and we can't change our life without changing our handwriting.

If we change a trait to change only the surface view of who we are, yet fail to change the belief system or behavior behind it, the trait will merely pop up to manifest somewhere else in the hand. The hand will always reflect the essence of the life.

It is similar to spiritual practice of affirmative prayer. We can't simultaneously be praying for prosperity and focusing instead on bemoaning our lack of abundance. We can't be praying for world peace and fighting with our spouse. Our lives are the single most obvious form of prayer in action. So when we counter in living what we pray in words and thoughts, which do you suppose prevails?

Handwriting behaves the same way. When we find ourselves saying one thing about what we believe and yet acting another, our handwriting will reflect the reality. Our digits will alter, our baseline wander, our signature stilt.

Yet if we change a belief system or behavior, that, too, will reflect in the hand. The whole interplay of who we are is intricately interwoven in the fabric of the being, always reflecting the essence of this being as represented by the *hand behind the word.*

7

Changing Your Handwriting
Changing your life

You can't change your Handwriting without changing your Life.
You can't change your Life without changing your Handwriting.

One of the most interesting things about handwriting is that it is both an input system and an output system. That is, we can examine it for how it reflects changes in our lives and we can change it and see how it reflects in our lives.

As the unique dynamic personal reflection tool that it is, handwriting can be used to model or monitor changes we desire to make in our lives by providing easy ways to take a sample and check to see how we're doing at any time. Let's touch on a few.

One of the techniques we use for sampling of handwriting changes is called a "check reading," where we review our own handwriting or the handwriting of someone we've seen before, comparing two or more samples and noting specific changes.

Some of the changes we notice may be changes undertaken to try to model changes in behavior or intention. Other changes may be some of the unintended consequences of making initial changes or may simply be the result of growth or recession of personality qualities along the way. The primary purpose of the check reading is to be able to observe handwriting changes and have a discussion about related personality and life patterns.

A question I am often asked in workshops and discussion groups is "If my handwriting suggests something about me which I don't really think is a part of my personality, can I change my handwriting to be more reflective of who I am?"

Certainly. Not only can you, but it is probably a good idea to consider doing exactly that. Often times especially younger people will have modeled their handwriting on mentors, elders, parents or someone whose handwriting they just liked. So it's entirely possible that in having done so they may have mistakenly agreed to carry marker traits which may not be reflective or healthy for them at this point in their life.

When we make changes in handwriting, we want to take into consideration how to do it and what the possible effect may be when we do it. These are not always obvious.

Certain handwriting changes are fairly easy to make yet can have a profound effect in our lives. Altering the forward or backward lean of the hand (slant), for instance, is linked to our willingness to lean into life or withhold our energy from it. The size of our handwriting is related to our self-concept, sense of who we are and our willingness to show up and be present in life's action plan. Changing these two and nothing more can be significant first steps to prove how changes in a hand can affect a life.

If these changes are made with an accompanying change in our intent to see them as our own, interesting patterns can emerge. People in our lives may comment on a change in our handwriting or they may comment on a change in our nature. Does the handwriting pull the life, or does the life pull the hand? Whichever the case, the two do interlink strongly enough to see these changes are made.

Consider doing a test exercise yourself to see how this works. Depending on what your handwriting looks like now, make a choice to alter its form to see what effects you notice in your life. For instance, if your handwriting is very small, set out to make it larger. If it is very large, try to make it smaller. Or if it is in between, you can play with slant, changing its lean back to the left if you lean right, or right if you lean left. For now, just see if you can feel the change. Once you've experienced the new hand for a few days or a couple weeks, you can decide if you want to make it more permanent. If you make a significant change in your hand you will almost certainly begin to feel the difference in your fingers, hand and arm while you write. The pen is apt to feel different.

In this day and age where many of us write by hand so much less often than we use computers, it may take a concentrated effort on your part to force yourself to do a reasonable amount of writing every day to reflect your changes. This you must do in order to help set these changes into your musculature and provide the necessary biofeedback link to your brain. Intention is half of the process but handwriting also requires action-oriented body motion to make it happen. The muscle feedback loop to your brain is the best way to do that.

When you are deciding what changes you could make, there are many different aspects of handwriting which are candidates. Each has a slightly different effect on the whole. Go back through the book and find some handwriting you like which you'd like to imitate or some like yours which you see has negative traits, and you'd like to change.

Here are some of the individual qualities of a hand we might change, arranged in approximate order of the greatest impact you could feel from making that change. Bear in mind, however, that some life patterns are much harder to change than size and slant:

- Mixed case (often difficult to change)
- General slant of the hand (right/left vertical tilt)
- Signature form and size
- Size of the general handwriting
- Readability / Neatness of the hand (hard to change)
- General slope of the hand (up down horizontal tilt)

Paul's Dilemma

I was recently asked by an eighteen year old student from another country we'll call Paul (not his real name) if I would help him change his handwriting to better reflect that he wanted to one day become a business leader or a top politician in his country.

Before speaking to me he had reviewed the handwriting of a number of business leaders and politicians from his country and the U.S. and had concluded that many of them wrote rather large with lots of gaps and sharp edges in their hand. So he decided that his tiny roundish handwriting shown here needed to be completely overhauled.

He set out to invent a new large, gapped, sharp-edged handwriting which he hoped would be more expressive of his desire to be more effective as a leader. The net effect was a rather fragmented and confused looking hand (seen on the next page) which he apparently had been very proud of until he spoke with me.

I didn't want to burst his bubble, but the handwriting he showed me seemed to have many problems. Although he is only eighteen, if I had seen this handwriting from someone I was looking to do business with, or looking to hire as an executive in my company, I would certainly have passed over this individual, no questions asked. He'd not even have gotten in the door for an initial interview.

Although he had some large cursive form in the hand, there were almost no letters touching any other letters anywhere except for an occasional oversized sinister sweeping hook in a "t" or "y" or "g" which made quite a spectacle of itself in the overall context and presentation of the hand. It definitely looked disturbed and might have had a bit of a psychotic air.

Needless to say, he was crushed when he heard that I not only didn't like his new handwriting, but strongly admonished him to immediately set about to change it significantly before people started to get the wrong impression about who he was.

143

Can you see why I would be concerned about his "new" hand? I think we could agree the original hand was too small and a little

Bigger is best
or better than this
1234567890
1234567890

wandering. It inhibited a healthy expression of who he is. But the new hand is perhaps too big and is definitely too strange. The sinister hook 't's and little heart shaped I-dots are too much! There are other things to worry about in this hand, too. His new 6 and "b" both are strange and unhealthy. It's just not comfortable.

Jerral at Eighteen

I remember going through a similar phase when I was eighteen. I definitely wanted to change my handwriting although I had no particular long-term professional ideas in mind like Paul about becoming a CEO of a major corporation or a top politician. I just knew that when I looked at my handwriting I could tell that it was not me. I felt that it needed to change to be more reflective of who I felt I was because it was interfering with my self esteem. When I looked at my handwriting I said to myself, "I don't like this guy. If this is me, then I want to be somebody else. Not him."

From behind the pen, behind the hand, it felt cramped and oppressed and I yearned to be able to be someone else.

I needed freedom of expression and creativity which I felt were not represented in the handwriting coming from my pen. Because it was not me, I needed to retrain it to better represent me. Here's a sample of my original:

I am still not satisfied
with this position in actually
1234567890   *Jerral*
1234567890   *Sapieza*

So I first set about to change my signature, then gradually more of my hand. Then within a few months of retraining of my hand to feel a bit more opened up and airy, I went on to look specifically at creating a new signature. I wanted something I could feel was more me, more open to growing and being more than the cramped confused person I was above.

To create a new signature, I took a sheet of paper and created three columns, then wrote from the top of the first column to the bottom of the page, then down column two, then down column three. With just over thirty rows on the page, I would have almost a hundred signatures on every page.

I did this for pages and pages until I had written hundreds and hundreds of signatures across several sheets of paper. When I was done with every page I would circle my three favorite signatures on that page, one from each column. I eventually started to see something I liked. I created a new "contrived" (as opposed to "evolved" or "borrowed") signature which you see in the second sample, on the next page. That one didn't last long, but it was an improvement.

An "evolved" signature is one which naturally emerges as our handwriting slowly changes over time from what we learned in school to how we most naturally write. A "borrowed" signature is one which has been adapted from a mentor, friend or other source.

We can see a more open hopeful playfulness in this second sample with a more natural dexter (forward) slant and a more natural gait to it. This fellow seems to be on the right track. I get a kick seeing that giant cover stroke there over my signature. It advertises a very self-conscious young man cautious about revealing who he is. Not exactly what we look for in a signature but it was who I was at the time. As I opened up, eventually that went away.

1234567890
Split the Atom when you
Fly the skies, walk upon
the moon . Use it!

Over the next few years into my twenties I again changed my signature a few more times until it settled at about age 25 and I arrived at more or less what my signature is today. If you're curious, see page 201 for a relatively recent sample of my handwriting.

The Parallels of Life and Handwriting

Like my own reasons for making a change in my hand, the changes Paul made to his hand reflect a confused young person in flux with some very conflicting needs who wanted to try stirring the waters to see what happened. On one hand his new hand says he is striving to make a statement about how confident and strong he is (improving the size of the hand the angularity of its occasional forward thrust). But at the same time, there is still a screaming little boy in there pleading with this new hand not to lose himself (the inflated I-dots' narcissistic focus; the fearful "s" and the imposed distance between every letter on the page).

Most psychologists seeing Paul's first hand, the tiny one, would have little trouble identifying significant self-esteem issues. But there are problems in over-compensating and going too large like his new hand as well. Tiny micro writing is usually the result of a writer's hesitance to "show up" and be present in his world. The over-inflated and oversized writing he has now is a very delicate balance of trying to pretend that he's okay and doing well when in fact the hand shows us very clearly that there are warning signs. Almost nothing is connected and the hand is clearly not a normal adult male's hand.

The micro writing, specifically when it has other problems in the hand, is one of the warning signs for a wound-too-tight, lack of self-esteem, marker of pre-violence which we can look out for most notably in teen boys. Rageful tempers often accompany this micro style of writing, because of the severe compression which forced it into its little box. Recall the mention of building blocks which went to building walls instead of bridges or roads? This is one of them.

When, like in Paul's case, an otherwise normal seeming young man exhibits such micro writing, it is usually a sign that his energy is being extremely compacted and compressed and is not coming out as communication. In Paul's case, his tiny writing is probably not surprising. His life has been one of relative privilege yet isolation because of his overshadowing and distant politician father.

Many teens in this situation find that attempts to get the father's attention have largely been answered by his aides or hired help and there is very little the child can do within normal bounds to get a reaction from the father. I applaud Paul's willingness and optimism to reach deeper and try something new to bring himself a sense of well-being, identity and presence rather than acting out in violence, anti-social or extreme behaviors to try to get his father's attention. My main concern is that the handwriting he chose to emulate is definitely not a functional one.

Paul's new hand does not even seem comfortable with itself. Notice how his strange 't's have to compete with each other for space because of their exaggerated shape and size. The 't's in this word "little" (which by the way is to scale here for the size of his new hand and decidedly not "little") have to fight for space in a way that make this neither a comfortable nor useful hand just yet. He agreed that there were things to work out but he did like these 't's.

Mindful Choice in Choosing a Hand

When we decide to change our handwriting, we need to be very mindful of the fact that choices we make for this social façade and public view of self will affect who we are, how we are perceived and how we function in society.

Our handwriting is a personal expression not only of the outer personality we offer to the world but of our inner turmoil and experience, our fears and hesitations, our emotional state and way of seeing the world. With so many interlocking pieces of the reflection it is very important that we be cautious before just wholesale adopting traits from someone else's handwriting.

It is like putting on their life as ours, slipping into their mind, their home, their most intimate clothing, relationships and beliefs and claiming them as our own. Certainly I would want to be very cautious about doing that. If we truly believe that handwriting speaks then we must also be willing to listen when it does, and take to heart its messages!

Changing the Cover Illustration

A case in point: the cover of this book. When cover designer Andy Kerr and I got together to discuss the direction of the cover he hit upon this "man behind the hand behind the word" design. We were both intrigued at the possibility. When I saw the first completed cover, I was stunned.

Andy had done his background research, read my book, even seen interpretations of some of the cover handwriting. But they were to him essentially just "inky squiggles on a page," useful for their composition density as a graphic design element, but little more.

Simply by the luck of the draw, Andy had somehow selected from the thousands of archived samples available, a sex addict, an abusive mother, a violent mental patient and a couple other unfortunate misfit samples to feature prominently in the cover design. Though I dearly loved the design concept, I knew we could not go to press with that offensive cover. It would have to be redone from scratch.

Poor Andy. It was his turn to be stunned. Understandably so. He had worked for days to create a superb design only to be told he would have to start again from scratch.

But with a pool of select samples he did exactly that and created a superb composition anew in the same form which invites and engages but in no way offends. I am happy to be warmly embraced there by friends and family and wonderful energy.

Like Paul who changed his signature by selecting pieces from random hands and incorporating them into his own, Andy had selected pieces from random hands and incorporated them into his expertly crafted design.

But when I saw the handwriting there, it spoke so loudly. I didn't see graphic images expertly placed in a design. I saw lives of abuse and abandonment, trickery and deception, molestation, addiction and offensive bravado staring back at me from the face on the cover of the book. The images were powerful, but I knew that it was time to do some changing of handwriting, changing a life.

It was a perfect reflection of this chapter's essence: that changing handwriting changes lives. Indeed it does, especially when the handwriting we change is the handwriting creating the opening image of the *man behind the hand behind the word*!

From the Other Side of the Table: Values, Mindset and Ethics

Although you may have already been looking at samples and speaking with people about their hands, this chapter is a bit less about technique and a bit more about the ethics and values of the handwriting analyst's work.

If we turn the tables and go around and sit on the other side of the desk, we get a feel for what someone else may experience as we work with them and their handwriting. Some of these points are common-sense interpersonal skills. Some are handwriting-specific issues you will want to consider. But all of them will make a difference to you and to the writers you will speak with in the course of looking at their handwriting.

Business Ethics in Handwriting Analysis

As handwriting analysis grows in popularity as a job screening tool for American business, there are some hard questions we need to ask before tumbling headlong into another messy business convolution. Corporations today already have a reputation for guiding their glide path primarily based only on the bottom line of profitability for shareholders. If handwriting analysis is presented only as a hiring process which provides business with a cost effective screening tool for peering secretly into the hidden lives of job applicants, then we've definitely missed the point.

It is true that in general, handwriting analysis can probably lower hiring costs by helping to better match people with jobs. And it is true that it is possible to use handwriting analysis to look at that *hand behind the word* and peer quietly into lives.

But if this clandestine third-party use is the only use business, government, schools or community organizations might propose for using handwriting, then I would be one to move for withdrawing from its use altogether.

There are ethical questions about the use of this technique or any other for peering insensitively and unapologetically into the lives of prospective employees as though they were mere cogs in a machine or cattle in a sorting chute. These are inappropriate uses of handwriting analysis. It is imperative to be respectful of the rights of people whose handwriting we see.

One reason I developed the *JAQS Style* sample format was so that samples in this format could be uniquely identified as samples collected specifically for the purpose of examination and analysis. No one is apt to write out this particular format of a handwriting sample without realizing that it is first and foremost collecting a sample for some purpose. Though they may not realize what all can be gleaned from such a sample without being told specifics, still they will realize it is likely a test or analysis of some sort.

In the right hands, a *JAQS Style* sample can provide a wealth of information about the writer, how they think, behave, create, argue, relate. In short, how the writer may fit into our team.

But in the wrong hands, or from the wrong ethical perspective, a handwriting sample can be just another weapon to brutishly wield against someone hit or miss, swinging carelessly and insensitively towards judgments of character traits, behavior patterns, education or life experience. It can provide an ignorant analyst with new vocabulary to alienate and damage trust and weaken relationships between all sorts of people. It is important that handwriting samples be used only wisely and well, respectfully and appropriately by those who understand their use and ethics.

We expect people in Medicine, Banking, Education, Law Enforcement, Human Resources and Training departments of our major corporations to conduct their day-to-day business with a modicum of ethics and good judgment. We expect them not to pry into personnel records or private histories for no apparent reason. We expect them to handle sensitive and private information they find with professionalism, tact and respect for privacy. In fact, there are federal and state laws governing these ethical issues.

But for the most part, unless they bump into laws governing privacy, libel or unfair hiring practices, there are no such laws which govern the use of handwriting by unscrupulous analysts who lay bare secrets to unscrupulous companies who employ them.

An Unethical Fishing Expedition

Whether an analyst can rightly point out a sense of depression or optimism or stress or creativity on this particular day from this particular sample is not the point. It must always be understood that handwriting is a dynamic and ongoing flow and not a set of personality traits set in stone for all time. Furthermore, it is not appropriate to use handwriting merely as a fishing expedition by analysts at the helm for employers snooping ethical waters they have no right to trawl.

There is a grave danger in allowing a company to have unfettered impersonal access to the state of mind or personality of an employee (impersonal in that it was gained not from interaction with the employee but from a third party's assessed judgment). It matters not whether the analysis is correct, or if it was only used purportedly as a technique to match the writer with some best possible job opportunity.

The legality of this kind of fishing expedition would not likely fly as an arbitrary infringement of privacy and it should not fly as a third-party assessed judgment, even from a handwriting analyst hired only to look at someone's handwriting.

Ethics in handwriting analysis should be of paramount importance for anyone considering its use. Yes, there are many personality traits, emotional states, historical events, desires, fears and aspirations which may well be seen even in a tiny sample of handwriting. But just because we see these things doesn't mean that we have a right to do with them whatever we choose or whatever a snooping employer chooses.

Unless there is a specific need for a company or agency to have specific behavioral information, such as that which may directly affect safety consideration for seniors or children in an individual's care, then personality traits seen in handwriting should not be passed back third-party to an employer for any use.

This is not to suggest that handwriting analysis should be muted in the traits it can see or report. There are quite literally hundreds of traits visible there to look at and report But whatever traits it is reporting should go directly to the writer of the sample and not to a third party. It is not the observation or awareness of intimate details in a hand which is the ethical violation. It is the passing on of any of this confidential information to a third party which causes the offending breach.

It is important that an analyst not be put in that untenable position of making an unwinnable choice between loyalty to a nosy employer paying the bills and loyalty to a writer's privacy.

The best of all possible choices where there is no contest between the employer and ethics is when the analyst is working not with the company, but with the writer directly.

Considerations for Sharing Directly with the Writer

Once it is possible to sit down and share directly with the writer of a sample, things can get much more interesting and enjoyable.

Although ethics will always be an overarching consideration in any discussion of handwriting, when sharing directly with the writer, there are other concepts we'll want to consider such as methods and techniques in personal and interpersonal communication.

A Smile and a Thank You Go a Long Way

Perhaps it seems a bit archaic to speak of smiles and thank yous, but they are a reality in interpersonal communication and still help people feel more comfortable with who you are. When you first sit down with a new person's hand, a thank you for their sample is a reasonable first engagement. You are indeed indebted to them for the offering of their sample from which you will learn.

The Three Gatekeepers

There's an Eastern mystics' saying attributed to Buddha which proposes that when you think about speaking, you should ask yourself three questions before ever opening your mouth:

First: **Is it True?** Of all the things we may consider about someone's hand, clearly all must first be true.

Then: **Is it Kind?** If we cannot speak kindly, then why would we want to utter anything at all? What purpose would it serve? Even if it is true, if it is not kind, why not just keep silent?

Lastly: **Is it Necessary?** There are already too many unnecessary words flying around cluttering up lives with misunderstanding. If we cannot contribute to a better understanding with this thought or idea, then best we leave it unsaid.

Before each of these gatekeepers every thought and idea must pass. Only those few which pass all three should be spoken. If this were the case, surely our world would be a quieter, wiser place. In your work as a handwriting analyst, I'd suggest we revise it just slightly in order to make it a bit more relevant to handwriting purposes:

Is it True?   A saucy sycophantic line, or making something up to fill the time is never useful or a good idea. Silence is better.

Is it Time?   Timing for handwriting is an important consideration. If we have no emotional history with the writer, some things we see may best be kept to ourselves because of intensity.

Is it Useful?   Does this serve this person's best interest for growth and reflection?" Though we may see something in a hand (like perhaps how extremely depressed the writer seems just now) saying this may or may not be useful at this time.

Mindfulness

It is important to take into consideration the nature of what you will be saying to someone and how it may be received and perceived. Bear in mind that there is truly a *hand behind the word*. This hand is, like all of us, a human being with feelings, emotions, fears, judgments and sensitivities.

Some people can be hyper-sensitive about their "stuff." In the event that you touch on something sensitive in the course of seeing what you see, you could open a floodgate of their pent up emotions. Not just emotions from this day and time, but emotions left over from childhood interaction with parents, teachers or authority figures across the years. You may touch on something and not even know it.

I have had people tell me how a conversation we had years ago about their handwriting (which I may or may not even recall) kicked off a whole series of events. Life hasn't been the same since, they tell me. Sometimes they have thanked me for the opportunity it gave them to grow. Sometimes they haven't perceived it as such a positive experience.

I cannot stress enough that people do listen when we're giving these handwriting readings. It is very important to err on the side of caution when touching upon sensitive personal issues. As a handwriting analyst, we have a responsibility to be truthful, compassionate and kind. It is important to be mindful of what we say and how we say it.

People may forget what we told them and they may forget what it meant. But they will not nearly so easily forget how we made them feel as we spoke with them about their handwriting. We must always be mindful of that little detail.

Case in Point: Admonitions Overlooked

Recently I was hired by a Fortune 100 company to do a handwriting training and discussion series for senior managers at their corporate headquarters.

At the dinner meeting on the final evening when I asked for discussion and questions, the senior manager spoke up and asked, "How often do people have to go to counseling after having spoken with you?"

At first, I thought she was kidding as did many others around the room, judging from their responses and laughter. But as I looked into her face I saw there a truly intense knitted brow and an earnest questioner. I recalled a conversation we had had a day earlier when in a private consultation I had spoken with her very frankly about some sensitive issues I saw in her hand.

That night as I answered, I told the group: Yes, indeed some times people do tell me they seek counseling as a direct result of our conversations about their hand. Not often, but occasionally.

The troubled look on the face of this manager continued to tell me that I had failed to take my own counsel of when to keep silent and when to speak, of when it is time and what is necessary. This was another powerful lesson for me.

Had I been too open and honest with her? Had my reflection been worded too strongly to be useful? Had I failed to take into consideration that although she was a senior manager, she was first a sensitive human being and would, just as any of us, still have feelings and fears and self-questioning doubts when a stranger sees secrets in her hand?

That evening was another wake-up call for me. I have been doing handwriting readings for almost thirty years, telling others about ethics and values and admonitions. Supposedly I know about the importance of what to say, whether to say it and how. Yet, clearly, it was again time for me to revisit those values.

I needed to remind myself to listen to my own words, to rethink what it looks like to be mindful and compassionate. Had I that week once again overstepped bounds and forgotten my core values? I had to quietly admonish myself anew: *What you say matters!*

What You Say Matters

I don't tell you these things to keep you silent as a handwriting analyst. I tell you to remind you, just as I still remind myself, that as keepers of these decoded messages of handwriting, we must be very careful how we share our vision and reflection with writers. They must feel we share with them as witness and not as reprimand. They must not feel judged or misunderstood.

It's not that everything in a handwriting sample is negative or harsh or difficult for people to hear. But most of us go through our lives quite unaware that the stripes and tics and quirky ways of our personality and experience have left such public marks in our handwriting, hanging out there in full public view for a stranger who happens to understand its message. It's usually not so much the negative as it is the private, which people find so threatening to have out there to be seen.

We need to be mindful and respectful of how we carry that torch and how we offer its light and heat back into their lives. You will make mistakes and learn your lessons. That is certain. There is no progress without the occasional mistake to temper a success. But ethics, etiquette and wisdom must always be tended whenever we are entrusted with working behind the scenes in the garden of these delicate fruits, from the *hand behind the word*.

9

Personal Relations & Compatibility Studies
Browsing Handwriting for Learning

One of the most useful applications of handwriting is that of helping people to better understand each other as they decide to consider a relationship. No doubt sometimes we feel we need all the help we can get understanding people. No matter whether you are a man or a woman, no matter what gender or age your partner, relationship almost always teaches us that we humans are infinitely complex creatures. Certainly we don't have to look at handwriting to know that.

But it's generally quite evident in the study of handwriting, too. As we might expect, the traits which suggest sensitivity and emotion tend to run more common in a woman's hand while the colder, more analytical hard-hitting points tend to run more common in a man's hand. There will of course be many exceptions.

More sensitive men will generally have more sensitive handwriting; more assertive and analytical women will have more assertive and analytical handwriting. It is not a fixed thing, that men or women have any particular reserved traits.

When I do presentations in college settings one of the questions I'm most commonly asked is "Can you tell anything about sexuality or sexual orientation from someone's handwriting?"

Here is a test for you. You will see more about these two men's samples again later in the chapter, one American and one German. We know these are both men. Do you suppose we can identify sexual orientation of either or both of these writers?

the first day rest of my life

"Ich weiß, was ich b *daß ich meine Fre*

20. Juni 1991

The question of sexual orientation is not one which can be easily determined by any sample. From so small a sample as these it is impossible to guess.

Human sexuality is a complex issue. Here we are in the early 2000's and the only thing we can agree about is that even today sexuality is a politically and socially charged issue with many taboos to boot.

We still have no definitive clarity about what defines sexual orientation or whether it is a biological, social, emotional or intellectual matter. Handwriting is influenced by and reflective of an individual's biological, social, emotional and intellectual makeup, so we might suspect that there could be some marker trait within gay and straight populations and all the gradations in between. But I have been sampling handwriting for decades with sample groups all across the spectrum and have not seen any clear evidence of a definitive marker for sexual orientation.

There are a number of other things which might show up in handwriting which could relate to relationship if we were asked to be on the lookout. Among them: devotion to a partner, argumentation style, fear of intimacy, open mindedness, loving respect for a partner, infidelity, lack of willingness to commit, domestic violence issues, dispassionate aloofness, relationships with coworkers, fear of intimacy and on and on.

There could be any one of a multitude of these or other relationship traits which one might see in handwriting, positive or negative, there for discussion. Certainly sexual orientation could come into any of these discussions. But again, from an ethical perspective, it would be imprudent and inappropriate to trawl into any of these relationship questions on a third-party fishing expedition.

Relationships That Work

Relationship is the single most popular thing people seem to want to talk about with handwriting. Whatever the gender of the partners, one thing we consistently see in relationships that work is a breadth of spectrum in their communication styles which tend to be more respectful, open and complete. Not only do they have an ability to inquire and play and discuss, but they also have an ability to strive for goals, create and move forward.

In studying success in relationship it doesn't seem to matter much which of the partners brings the necessary communication skill to the partnership nor what is the gender of the partner. The important thing is that if the broader spectrum is present, the relationship has a better chance of succeeding. The handwriting of a compatible couple will usually reflect compatible wholeness.

When couples tend to be shorter spectrum overall, that is, if they're both hot headed self-starters or both extremely sensitive and artistic but lack drive and commitment, troubles ensue.

For instance, competition and combativeness can tend to be constant and demanding (for the fiery driven competitive couples) and a constant blaming and whining and lack of accomplishment can loom forever in the wings for the couple who are both sensitive artistic dreamy types, but lack the fire.

A pleasant overall sense of well-being and resolution is most common among couples who specifically choose to keep their communication open with compatible styles between them.

Hurried or Quick?

Couple compatibility in handwriting is almost a lifetime study in itself. To touch on some of the possibilities of what works and what doesn't let's start by looking at individuals and the traits which make them up. To begin with, let's look at a difference between quick and hurried. By quick we usually mean a speedy hand written by an engaged and thinking mind: an efficient, flowing hand which basically glides across the page. A quick hand doesn't usually appear rude, impatient or lacking in readability. It will generally indicate a good communicator in relationship.

The hurried hand can often seem harsh and rude. Hurrying usually means shortcuts in detail are taken, so the hand usually suffers in appearance. It often has a feel of fury and impatience since the writer didn't take the time to be mindful of details in the writing nor mindful of the reader's ability to understand. These writers are generally not very good at communication in relationship because they either haven't learned how to take the time, or they are choosing not to.

Look at the following two samples and decide: which seems like a flowing quick mind and which seems more hurried, which one seems more sensitive and which one harsh?

> True ... Nervous, very, very dreadfully nervous I had been and am! But why will you say that I am mad?

> I met Ferral in a coffee shop in front of the Eugene City Jail.

Can you see that the one on the left is probably more quick and flowing and the second one is more hurried? The second one has some harshness in its form. Although it may seem fast and hurried, it is not efficient at all.

A flowing efficient hand typically feels more pleasant, gentle and appealing. Inefficient letter breaks in a hand like this contribute neither to its readability nor its appeal. Notice the places where this writer decided to break words and how she started and terminated words. It seems very haphazard and inefficient. For instance: the word "met" is made by writing "me," breaking and then coming back to make and cross the "t."

True ... Nervous, very, very dreadfully nervous I had been and am! But why will you say that I am mad?

I met Ferral in a coffee shop in front of the Eugene City Jail.

Then the strange hooked "J" starts, but in order to make that odd shaped "J", she has to start at the top, come down, hook back to the left, then back to cross the top of the "J." Very inefficient.

Then the word "coffee." There are extra loops in the "o and the two "f's" were made as individual characters, disconnected from the rest of the word completely. The strange "E" and "g" in Eugene are also very inefficient strokes.

This version of "fast writing" is in reality, not very fast or efficient at all. This is probably a very confused mind with too many things going on and she may not even realize she's doing it. Can you feel the impatience in this hand?

The first sample was probably written almost as quickly as the second one, probably faster, but has a completely different feel. It is flowing, pleasant and likely the product of a quick creative well-nurtured being. It is not impatient. Even though her words say she is nervous and wonders if she is mad, (though of course as an analyst we're not reading these words at all, are we?) she is very easy and free-flowing about how she writes.

But this second one, can you feel its edginess and resentment? It has several places where there are what we call "sinister" hooks in it, meaning that they hook back to the left. Sinister strokes are not efficient strokes because they tend to quite literally walk back over themselves and interfere with a natural forward flow of the hand. They are common in emotional people with a history of resentment and anger issues learned in childhood from having to unreasonably defend every position.

Notice the sharp edges on the "m's" and "r's" and "n's." These suggest impatience and insensitivity. The odd "J" hooks are similar again. They are particularly sharp and insensitive and tend to suggest rebelliousness. Certainly these are not the "J's" we are taught to make in fourth grade handwriting class. Usually a "J" has a gentle flowing friendliness to it but this one's friendly form was compromised by its sharp sinister hook and its excessive and sharp cover stroke, especially in "Jail." If we would like to know more about this second one, then we can take a look at some of the digits from the sample. We might ask, "Why is she so defiant about standard form in her writing? Is she rebellious or careless or does she just not realize what's normal?"

Traits in the Digits

When we see the digits we do register carelessness, noting that she started to make a 7 following the 5 and the shape of many of her digits is irregular and uneven. But it's more than just carelessness. She simply can't be bothered to take the time. There's an uneven wandering baseline and variations of height all through the digits. Look at the compression in her 8's (sense of major traumas in life). She is probably burdened quite heavily with emotional stresses just now.

Her 2's have a trait known as the spaghetti 2, because it looks rather like it was just tossed onto the page like spaghetti on a plate:

1 2 3 4 5 6 7 8 9 0
1 2 3 4 5 6 7 8 9 0

uneven and lacking a definitive shape. 2's have to do with how we form relationships, our impersonal view of others. Hers suggest a detachment from people, causing her frustrations, never quite knowing how to make initial contact.

The upper right of her 7 is sharp and well cornered. That's good. But the angle is a bit too tight with the top of the seven too downward. We like to see a sharp corner on a 7 since a sharp corner tends to mean that this is a person who is willing to take a principled stance and stand up for what she believes in. But that "too tight" angle of the 7 is one of the signs of excessive emotional stress and can reflect a hair-trigger temper, especially when accompanied by a 6 like that one next door. Its wide flat loop and short stem are another indication of a temper brewing.

Whether we look at the digits or the words in this hand, we see here a wounded, driven, resentful hand which probably is not a temporary state of being, but has something to do with her upbringing. She could probably tell some sad, tough stories.

Sensitivity

The fact that this is a woman's hand is one of the things which makes it unusual and stand out more. Women usually tend to have softer, more sensitive, gentle handwriting. They tend to be able to be competitive and stand their ground and push forward in business and other arenas in life with the best of their male counterparts, yet at the same time able to maintain more readable and sensitive handwriting than most men's.

So when a woman's hand is so sharp and harsh and rough looking like this, there is usually a reason. We can guess that she is perhaps currently under a great deal of stress or has deeper ongoing wounds as a result of her past or upbringing.

We notice that men's handwriting is different, though we can't always necessarily predict why. As we discussed earlier, it could be hard wired genetics, could be socialized machismo, could just be obstinate lack of willingness to be artistic and sensitive. Sociologists are still working on these big questions and will be getting back to us! But in the meantime, men's handwriting does often tend to be harsher and less sensitive than women's.

the first day
rest of my life

„Ich weiß, was ich bi
daß ich meine Fre

20. Juni 1991

So let's take a look now at those men's writing and see what we see. If we use some of the same criteria we used for the women's we should be able to pick out the more sensitive of these two. Which hand seems more sensitive and flowing, round and balanced, in short, open minded and free?

Perhaps you'd like to start with an easier question: One of these is the son of scientists who worked on the Manhattan Project and one is the son of rural pig farmers in northern Germany. Any idea which is which? (I thought you deserved an easy question before we get into some of the more difficult ones!)

The Official Forensic View of Handwriting

Before we talk more about these two men's hands, you may find it interesting to learn that the forensic guidelines offered by the Federal Bureau of Investigation a few years ago as their official statement of the FBI's stance regarding handwriting says that we can never determine gender, age or specific personality traits of a writer from a handwriting sample. I am not sure that I agree with this position, although I understand why they make it.

Their point could be used to underscore what I said earlier about there being a wide spectrum of variation in handwriting. They also, however, push a little further and say that there are no specific marker traits for a uniquely male or female hand. But to say that we can *never* make a determination of gender, age or specific personality traits on the basis of a handwriting sample seems to push the issue a little far into the realm of "it's not black and white and therefore does not exist." I tend to respectfully disagree.

Men in general are not known for having sensitive handwriting. Often cursive handwriting is more flowing and sensitive. But just because a writer chooses cursive, it does not always follow that the cursive is sensitive. These two samples make exactly that point.

If we ask which of these seems to be more sensitive, what we look at to make a determination will be the structure of the characters which are typically more round or flowing. Softer and more round usually means more sensitive. If, where we expect to see round, the characters are pointed or angular, that's probably a personality with sharper edges.

In the German one, by the way, those are not "B's." Don't judge him for throwing in a capital B at the end of a word! The words *weiß* and *daß* are supposed to look like that. In German the ß takes the place of a double "s" and being the nicely rounded form it is, it is useful for us to look at to help make the determination in this context.

So which one did you come up with as more sensitive and gentle?

We'd probably find the German sample more sensitive. The American one has some strange letter formations with a tendency to leave out parts of certain simple letters (like "h" and "y") while misshaping and over-drawing others ("d", "a") So as it is, it comes out jerky and angular. Not flowing. What's that about? For now, let's just say probably it's not about the sensitivity we're looking for.

Sensitivity usually has a softer more pleasant form to it. Clearly, of these two, the German is more sensitive. This ability to identify sensitivity through roundness and softness in handwriting is usually one of the easiest traits for people to be able to see first, especially when it is a matter of choosing which of a pair is more sensitive. It is usually not so difficult to identify what is more round and what is more angular in handwriting.

That's because, being a writer yourself, you know where loops generally occur and where they don't. So what feels more round, looped, softer and sensitive is in a way just feeling the words as they're written and feeling which seems more natural.

PS: Regarding our writers from the first of the chapter and the question about their sexual orientation: these are both gay men, though I doubt that you'd ever guess it from their hand.

Just Digits

So what happens, then, when we look at some handwriting without any words or letters? Can we still figure out when we have no words or letters to work with, but have instead only the digits?

Since we just looked at a couple of men's handwriting with the last set, let's look at a couple of women's hands now. These two rows of digits are from several years ago, two women writers, one a twenty-something writer and the other a nineteen-year old college student.

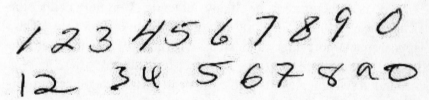

These two writers don't know each other but for the sake of examples let's assume they were friends and figure out how they would communicate. A good place to start is with the same kind of clues we used for letters and words in the previous sample. We know the general shape of the digits as we write them. So if we look at the digits in the form they're written here, which one feels more naturally rounded, sensitive and pleasant looking?

If we look only at the 2, the lower one probably seems more pleasant. It has a softness about it with a long swooping tail and gentle turns. But if we look at the rest of this line of digits something is wrong here. The 2's tail is a bit too long in this context and there is a giant space after it. Remember that from two previous samples? This tells us that this 2 is probably pretending something. In this case, pretending to be more sensitive than it really is. Since it is the only one of the digits with such a swooping characteristic and since there is that large space after it, it is probably not an authentic digit for this hand. It is trying way too hard to make sure we see it.

Pretense, hesitation and deception in handwriting often is related to exaggerated form and odd spacing between letters or numbers. In this case, the gentle loop and swooping stroke of the 2 is indeed a nice touch. But it is a bit overdone and followed by that huge gap and a decidedly unimpressive 3, a completely different form.

This 2, therefore, is not likely authentic. Certainly neither the 3 nor the 9 or 0 has this kind of communicative form to it. They appear much more angry and harsh. Why angry? Because there are typically strokes inherent to a 3, 9 or 0, for instance, where there is a rounded sweeping form. Those are nearly completely absent from this hand.

There is no rocker base on the 3, there is no rounded form at all to the top; the normally round part of the 9 is almost closed up and compressed; the zero is not very round at all. Especially for a female, these are quite harsh and angular strokes where generally we might expect to find rounder softer ones.

The balanced spacing of the top sample could suggest that it would be at least a bit more consistent and so might be more respectful of others. But there are some extra little strokes in the 1, 2, 5, 8, all of which harden or sharpen this hand. The exaggerated pushy right slant is troublesome for truly being communicative. This hand is not a very good choice either. Now we're really in a quandary! So which is it?

I didn't really mean to throw in a trick question, but all in all, neither of these seems very workable. Neither one of them passes the harshness and distance question. Disruptive spacing, excess tics and hooks, malformed characters and inconsistencies in a hand all contribute to a feeling of harshness and insensitivity and all inhibit communication. But good lessons to learn from.

By the way: could you perhaps guess which of these women is a political activist? Which might you think? Think about the fact that politics is not a place for the squeamish. Which one seems to have an ability to do some real fighting while at the same time appear to have a genuine smile on her face all the while?

Probably that second one, the one with the long tail on that 2. The 2 says she can reel 'em in with the smile and then "*ZAP!*" let the other steam-roller digits take over for dealing with harsher realities. She works out her deals, then back on the street with her smile, she takes on another challenge and starts the process all over again.

Sorry about the complication of this one. Although it seemed like a trick question, I assure you it was not originally intended that way. I guess neither of these was exactly a poster child for a sensitive hand of artistic serenity and communication.

Let's do one to make up for that. Here is one with very little distraction or strangeness to it, very little room for doubt that it is a gentle open hand. Can you see and feel the sensitivity here? This is one which practically oozes with sensitivity all the way through it.

1 2 3 4 5 6 7 8 9 10

No argument here, is there? This hand is female, too. She's a visionary sculptor and artist, with talents and interests in many different fields including architecture, theology, end-of-life caregiving and foreign languages and cultures. You can probably tell she has a far more gentle form throughout than either of the two above. Kind, thoughtful, smiling. Not hurried, not too slow.

Can you *feel* the openness to communicate? A communicative sensitive hand will generally have a full-form richness to it instead of taking shortcuts. Round segments will be full and round. Straight lines will be consistent and direct.

1 2 3 4 5 6 7 8 9 10

Recall the spaghetti 2 from a few pages ago. One of the objections to that one was that it did not have the definitive corner and loop in it. This sample, while not getting carried away and overdoing the roundness and loops, still satisfies all the basic criteria of form for a 2 and does so pleasantly.

Can you feel that? Does your intuition help you to see and feel the artist in this sample? Ideally, that is the direction we'd like you to be able to go, to start to automatically *feel* what a hand represents. If you're not quite there yet, don't worry about it. You'll get there.

For now, let's look at a few more single strings of digits for comparison and contrast, similarities and differences so that you can get used to identifying patterns. Ideally, in explaining things to you, if you are given a discussion of a particular stroke or pattern to look for, you should be able to identify which of the samples best exemplifies or relates to that form. Many of the following traits are strong if not negative ones but that doesn't mean we only see negative things in people's handwriting. For beginners, though, they're usually more interesting. Let's see how this goes:

Standing Up and Taking a Stance

Let's start with a trait of being willing to take a stance, make a point, stand up for position. The main components of this sort of trait will be sharper corners where digits have corners (lower left of 2, upper right of 7, sharper boxed corners of the 4, etc). and in addition, the hand will also usually have a fairly strong lean to the right, symbolizing that it leans into life, standing by its convictions and choices.

1234567890

1 2 3 4 5 6 7 8 9 0

So then, which of the two women above would you expect to be more decisive and willing to express herself? Both have the lean, so that's good. When you look for the sharper corners what do you see? Should be pretty clear.

The lower one is more willing to take a stance and speak up about what she wants, needs, believes. Notice the sharpness in her 2's, 4's. In this case, both have relatively sharp 7's so that's not going to help us make a determination. Good to know they both have it. But with the lower one's 2, 4 and 7 compared to just the 7 above, we have a clear winner there.

The second sample is also more opinionated. The trait I mentioned in the introduction to the book about a 7 tic shows up in the lower woman's sample and in these two 7's. It has to do with a tic in the upper left of a digit. The tic in the sample above is not very pronounced, so I'll show you another couple for more clarity.

77

The 7 on the right also has a stress foot which means that this trait is currently burdened or stressed. The horizontal cross stroke on a 7's center, by the way, does not really mean much other than that this person probably studied foreign languages or science and learned it there. If it's there, we look at where and how it crosses and read it similar to a t-bar.

One-on-One Compatibility Studies

Let's look now at a series of four rows of digits, all four of whom have a rather strong temper which rumbles quite a long time before blowing, but which nonetheless blows very high when it does. This is usually the result of severe ongoing emotional stress. It generally shows up as a stab into the center of the 8 or 0, or both, and usually has the "double snowball 8's" formed by two stacked circles. Snowball 8's usually mean power and control is a big issue to the writer.

If you met any one of these people you'd think they were charming and pleasant. For the most part, temper issues probably would not be something we would expect from them because of their demeanor. But that's where handwriting comes in handy!

1 2 3 4 5 6 7 8 9 0

1 2 3 4 5 6 7 8 9 0

1 2 3 4 5 6 7 8 9 0

1 2 3 4 5 6 7 8 9 0

The top two are female, bottom two are male, all early twenties. For the sake of discussion you may want to know that the women are best friends and the guys don't know each other but if they did they'd probably be good friends, too. I just pulled them together for their similar traits. One common trait they all have is intensity.

Intensity

The intensity starts in those snowball 8's. It's also in the pressure with which each wrote (which is a little hard to reproduce unless you can see the original and feel the nice reverse contour on the back of the page). Pressure with which someone writes is one of the strongest indications we can have of intensity in a hand. By itself intensity is neither positive or negative. If it's coupled by creativity, for instance, it can be delightful. If it's accompanied by a temper, however, it can get dangerous sometimes.

The Women

1 2 3 4 5 6 7 8 9 0
1 2 3 4 5 6 7 8 9 0

1's: The lower one has a taller sense of self. Top's 1 is too small.

2's: The top has a fairly gentle pleasant view of society, but not exactly optimistic (tail would go up). She's also open minded: a full and uncluttered roundness to her 2. Compare with the lower one, who loves to talk to people, (full loops in the 2) and is a pretty good listener (shape of the 2 looks like an ear) though she tends to judge (tic and loop in 2 top) and is a bit cynical (little frown in the tail).

3's: They both have a slightly sinister (left leaning) slant to their 3's suggesting that they tend to withhold commitment at work. But the top's rocker base is a little fuller. She's probably more effective as an employee.

4's: The top one is more open to relationship (open top 4) but less driven, unlike her friend whose 4-tail goes well through the stem. Lower's tight triangle means picky about relationship.

5's: They both tend to be playful and fun, as we can see from the playful looking 5's. But the bow in the top of the lower 5 says she hates time pressures, so is probably late more often. Sense of humor is probably more brash (left lean and open bottom).

6's: Both have small sized loop in the 6. That means neither has much tolerance or patience with the small stresses of life like someone stealing all the paperclips or eating the last doughnut. The lower is more apt (rightward lean) to speak up and have to let you know what she thinks (that little tongue going through the bottom of the 6).

7's: This is a place where big differences start. Notice the top one's quiet little 7 up there almost apologizing for having an opinion. Not so with the lower one! Apologizing is probably not in her

1 2 3 4 5 6 7 8 9 0

1 2 3 4 5 6 7 8 9 0

nature. She has a huge tic on the upper left of her 7, indicating that she just has to speak up and tell people what she thinks whether they asked for it or not. We call that the "exporting of principles" stroke. Unlike her upper friend, notice the stress foot of the 7, too. It is bent and ticked, suggesting that even she finds her principles a burden.

8's: Probably major childhood traumas with both these young women (actually with the guys, too). They all have misshapen and stabbed 8's. That usually means abuse or abandonment or both. They seem confused and conflicted about what happened to them as children (misshapen and stabbed 8's, larger top circle than bottom and sinister slant).

This could even be a part of how they happen to be such close friends, having bonded from similar childhood trauma (each has the other half of the velcro). Only another intense snowball 8 type person will tolerate so much picking, suspicion, argumentation, control as they each work through their difficulty. It gets complex.

9's: Their 9's are remarkably similar for being different writers. Both full world view (O) and short self view (|). They both seem very interested in professional interests but lack confidence there. At the time of the samples, they were both full-time students and only working part-time.

0's: The zeroes both have a mistrustful stab to the heart at their center but they're both well-rounded and observant.

Of these two women overall the second is the more intense and driven and will probably go far, once she works out all the angst and stress in her life. With all the energy and intensity she has, she would be well advised to put it into art, music or self expression of some kind. She could be a tremendous success one day.

The Men

1234567890

1234567890

1's: Our top guy's 1 is rather large. Actually all of his digits are good sized. He's probably confident and a bit cocky, too. We'll see more details on that all the way through. His friend below has a tiny little 1. He probably admires the top guy, but might find him overpowering. Big difference in the size of their 1's.

2's: The spaghetti 2 on top has no real clarity in the corners. He likes to keep things moving and doesn't like to commit. Look at the tail of the 2: It's a much lighter stroke than the rest and short. His friend below, however has a nice upper hook on his 2. It's like a full ear shape which means he's a good listener. It does have the little frown in the lower loop, though. He is cynical and doesn't have much faith in people's ability to actually be there for him following through with their commitments. The top guy is exactly the kind of person he'd find annoying. Notice that spaghetti 2 up there which promises the world but just doesn't deliver. It's that salesman thing. The top fellow's detached impersonal 2 doesn't listen and won't get involved. For people like the dedicated listener below, this must be frustrating.

Slope: One of the first things which stands out about the slope of these two rows of digits is that they are very much opposites. But it's the velcro thing again. With their 8's and 5's and 6's and 0's so similar, they would probably be very good candidates for being best friends. The top has trouble with mania (his digits are oversized for his writing with an overt up slope). He tends to always be a little too happy and though he's a genuinely sweet man, he can drive people nuts bouncing off the walls having so many ideas and talking like a salesman. The bottom, on the other hand, is just the opposite. He is cautious and kind, tending toward depression and hesitance to act around people, (small

1, downward slope of the digits, uneven base) though he works well alone (full top of the 3). The two probably would annoy each other a bit but they are also very much soulmates and should appreciate each other's talents and skills for looking at life in a suitably complementary way.

3's: They are different but complementary again. Notice the upper has a nice full rocker base on his 3 which means that he tends to go above and beyond the call of duty when it comes to work and neighbor relations. But then look at his friend's 3. Tends to be a very hard worker (top part of the 3 has a canopy to it and that inner shelf at the middle of the 3 is very firm) though again a bit cynical or downward sloped with the 3 at its base. That base says he's cautious about putting in too much of his cooperation with others for the whole if others aren't contributing. With the fullness of the top of his 3, he's always working hard. Just that it might not be toward the team's stated goals. His chum above is always playing cheerleader for the team's goals (rocker base) but operates more on autopilot than really working hard (center shelf of the 3 is weak).

4's: 4's tell us about intimacy, sexuality and our private relations. At the time these samples were taken, it appears neither is in a relationship or if they are they are not being satisfied. The little left leg and cross stroke of the 4 is weak and small.

A 4 has three separate segments: the self (tall downstroke) the partner (the shorter leg downstroke) and the relationship itself (the cross stroke).

For the upper young man, relationship is another place to have an upbeat but detached view. Notice the slope of the cross stroke of the 4 is exactly parallel with the tail of the 2. Neither his 2-tail or 4-cross is full of energy. For our bottom, the size of the 4 is quite small. He's not very confident in relationship. His friend's detached bravado (big but empty 4) might be attractive to him as a wishful way he might dream he could do it.

5's: The boys are both pretty playful. The playful rocker bases on the 5's show they have good senses of humor, but different. Top one has the full salesman rocker base again, as in his 3's. The lower has a tighter-wound sense of humor, probably more a giggle than a belly laugh. Belly laughs usually have a full rocker base with the bottom part of the 5 taking up full width and more than half of the height of the 5. This one is only about 60% width, probably 40% of the height.

6's: These get interesting here, for how these two guys would get along with some stress. 6, as you may recall, is the way we deal with the minor irritations of life. Both have almost identical shaped 6's, but the lower is smaller and has a greater dexter (rightward) lean. Therefore he becomes the one more willing to discuss those minor traumas and work them through. The friend above doesn't like to deal with these things. His sinister (leftward) lean says that. It doesn't really seem to fit with some of his other digits; the digits up to here have been quite forward slanted but with the 6 and 7, his confidence droops.

7's: Here, too, the lower excels. Notice his nice tall sharp-cornered 7. We like to see that. The fact that it is the tallest staff of the four main staffs (1, 4, 7, 9) says that he actually tends to define himself by his principles and it's something he gives a lot of thought to. He knows his principles better than he knows himself (1) or his idea of relationship and intimacy (4) or his profession (9).

Contrast that with our top. His 7 staff is actually the shortest of the four (1, 4, 7, 9) and has a stress foot on it (the little bend at the bottom). The stress foot says principles are something he considers a burden at the time of this sample; he's just not comfortable.

8's: Like the women, both of the guys have their childhood wounds here showing as a knot in the center of the 8's (and a bit in the 0's) where there is a very similar knot at the top. The 8's and 0's would be a place where these guys would feel a real sense of camaraderie and

1234567890
1234567890

understanding for each other's childhood.

Both have the control-oriented snowball 8's so would both be rather tenacious about any new traumas and dramas they might create together in the friendship. They'd also both gravitate toward drama (in their lives, not on stage), with those inner 8 tangles and that knot or scab just to the top left of their 0, which is almost identical.

9's: Look how tall and proud the top's 9 staff is. He's very confident about his role in the world. It is literally likely to be a role for him, as though he were on-stage acting his life. Our friend below is much more tentative and quiet, even burdened in his 9 (stress foot). It tends to be the lowest point on his baseline.

Ironically, Lower's commitment to work hard at his job (top of the 3) is the highest point in the most upper zone of his digits and his sense of self (1) is the highest on the baseline. Those three things together would suggest that he must have some identity questions about his role in his job right now.

0's: The knot or scab in both's 0's speaks of a knotted challenge in their teen years which affected their world view (0). It's in their teens because they're both in their early 20's and it's slightly to the left of the top of the 0. Top of the 0 would be current; right is future, left is past. So the knot is relatively recent, but strong.

These seem to be twin souls here. For people who live in different states and have never met, these guys are very similar in the shape of their 6's and 0's. It's that other half of the velcro thing again!

So that's the digits' story of how these two would get along. How are you doing with your ability to feel the essence of what those examples meant? Do you feel like you might be ready to make more sense of these things? Is handwriting starting to feel like something you can understand?

As you take more samples of your own from people in your world it's apt to make even more sense as you start seeing some patterns up close and personal.

The commitment to learn about handwriting begins a new way of looking at life for many people. Often as they start out, though, they don't yet trust their wisdom to know what they see. If you are doubting your wisdom and vision looking at examples here, I hope you will begin to trust that as you look at more and more handwriting, you will begin to be right more and more of the time. Trust your genius. Be open to its gift. Or if you can't yet trust your genius, then at least be open to its dull suggestive thud reminding you that you might be getting in the way of your own wisdom!

Think how fascinating: All these stories from only two rows of digits in two sets of hands. The bulk of this chapter's story of personal relations and compatibility was told only in digits.

There's a lot of information there. As you begin to trust your ability to see these things, you will find that you don't always need to see the printed words to begin to hear the emergent whispers of the handwritten life stories around you.

Next time someone scribbles a note and hands you only a phone number on a slip of paper, take a moment to see it. Feel first the *gestalt* of its story. Smile and open to your wisdom. Then see the digits on the page for what they truly are: the combination to a vault this person is welcoming you to open, as the two of you share more secrets there, in this *hand behind the word.*

10

Handwriting Analysis for People Managers
Using Handwriting in the Workplace

People in supervisory or managerial roles, whether in business, education, service organizations or the clergy all have something in common. Their ability to function as an organization depends in part on how effectively they demonstrate the values and principles the organization holds and how well they understand their people.

Managers who hire only people like themselves will eventually start to find themselves in a stagnant dysfunctional organization. Organizations need variety, diversity and new blood in order to grow with new challenges. One of the useful applications of handwriting in an organizational development setting is to help determine a candidate's personality match with an organization's culture.

This may mean seeing if a candidate is like the organization now or it may mean seeing if a candidate can perhaps broaden an organization's base of skills, resources and compatible diversity by reaching for new traits to include in the search.

One good place for handwriting to help out in the hiring process is when large pools of applications are on file for a limited number of positions. After a meeting with hiring managers to discuss needs and expectations of the ideal candidate, an analyst can then usually help make some initial determinative cuts fairly quickly.

Using the requirements and expectations of a particular position, it should be possible to quite easily sift and sort applicants into two sets, either fitting or not fitting the match criteria.

Keeping in mind the job requirements and looking only at applicants' handwriting, an astute analyst will be able to, in a matter of minutes, pare down a stack of dozens of applications into those who would likely fit and those who would not.

In addition to using handwriting to pare down a stack of applications, it is useful for day to day reflection on personalities and team interaction or general reflection for business contacts. This might best be devoted to an entire book in itself, but let's look at overviews of using handwriting in a people management context.

Using Elemental Shape and Overall Form of Characters

Depending on the nature of the requirements for a position, here is one set of criteria which allows for some quick discernment of an applicant's handwriting by assigning it to one of four basic elements: Air, Earth, Fire or Water.

You will see more on the elements in Chapter Twelve but here we'll delineate them in a job context.

Original, Varied, Thin or Random (Air)

Can tend to be fragmented and idealistic. Very creative, but not always good at finishing tasks or tending a clock or budget. Often talks to self while working. Can be chatty. Is extremely flexible and adaptable to change. Can make conversation with just about anyone, no script necessary. Distractible. Can have trouble focusing on a single thing; sees order and structure as a cage. Very difficult to offend; very unlikely to offend unless caged. Able to function and add value in just about any capacity or position for short periods; usually willing and eager to learn new tasks. Loves to do anything; doesn't always do everything well. Make great temporary employees, contractors.

Squarish with Full Middle Zone (Earth)

Tends to be a realist, committed; can be stubborn and resistant to change. Usually excellent producer when directions are understood and clear. May have trouble stopping once they get going, in work or play. Can take a concept and flesh it out to full production. Not so good at creating the initial spark, but very good at tending the fire and making excellent use of its resources. Thrifty and appreciative of beauty and value, very good at keeping tasks on budget. Love to laugh heartily and enjoy good food and sensual pleasures. Can over-indulge if not moderated. Rarely forgets; can hold a grudge forever.

Sharp / Jagged, Intense (Fire)

Prefer to lead rather than follow, regardless of actual position in an organization. Can be problematic to manage. Extremely creative and competitive. Can be opinionated, garish and harsh. Aren't troubled to always analyze their own situation (or anyone else's accurately). In the right position like Sales, Marketing, Development they can be powerhouses. Excellent visionaries and creative starters; not always so good at follow-through. Willing to confront and take on most any challenge but may need an emotional cleanup team following them around fixing damaged relationships or social gaffes. Thick skinned and able to endure tough times, struggles and temporary downturns like a trooper. Can motivate others (and sometimes abuse others) with ease. Extraordinarily creative and so can be given to complex fantasies of reputation or paranoia. Not always ethical, but when guided well can blast new territory open very quickly. Can be fiercely competitive and defensive when thought to be misunderstood.

Roundish With Full Middle Zone (Water)

Tend to deal with life emotionally; sensitive and observant, thoughtful and often quiet until actively engaged. Usually excellent with people and people problems. Can tend to be moody. Not so much a doer or a producer as catalyst and motivator. Can be very intuitive and able to bring out the best in others. Need more hands-on management in order to avoid feeling dreamy, depressed or misunderstood. Need to talk out their situation and feelings to best succeed. Can be secretive and cautious; not usually fond of being in sales or on stage.

Some of the Basic Points to Always Look For

Although it's difficult to present a prescription for exactly how to go about choosing any applicant for any job, there are a couple of traits an analyst might be looking to universally include or exclude for any job. For instance, honesty is one of those traits most jobs would probably include. Social deviance is one of those traits most jobs would likely avoid. Lucky for the dishonest and social deviants of our society, however, not all employers can even identify these traits!

- Is it neat?
- Is it readable?
- Is it pleasing to your eye?
- Is it familiar to you?

Some of these are quite subjective. But common sense does help you when you're looking at handwriting. As a hiring manager, you probably already have at least a basic appreciation of familiarity. But be careful; it can also get you into trouble if you act only on that familiarity hunch. Just because handwriting is familiar doesn't mean anything more than that you will probably develop a quicker more familiar rapport with this person (which isn't necessarily bad) like you have developed with others in the past.

But familiar rapport could be the familiar way you always fight with your Uncle Joe, or it could be the familiar way you always fall in love at the wrong time for the wrong reasons. Familiarity in itself simply means this person is in your group of Life's Teachers!

You will also want to be wise enough about handwriting to be able to determine "neat" from "overly neat." Why? Because as you will recall from Chapter Four, overly neat handwriting often tends to mean that the writer is pulling the wool over your eyes and trying to hide something less attractive from you. Some of the best liars and embezzlers in the world can write in ways which may appear to the untrained eye to be very neat, in fact, *too* neat!

Embezzlement's Relationship with Being Neat

Those most likely to want to steal from you will usually have handwriting which hits one of the two pegs of the neatness scale, overly neat or overly messy. Perhaps surprising to many people, it's the overly neat writers who make the best embezzlers. It's also usually those with the overly neat handwriting who are rarely the internal suspect. Their supervisor says of them, "Oh, no, they would never steal from us! Completely loyal, long time great employee." Oh, okay. Hmm. They've got your number.

Recall that embezzlement is essentially a confidence game. The fact that you are so certain that this person's handwriting is so neat that they would never steal from you is one of their games. You have successfully fallen victim to their con and bitten the bait if you like their writing. To you, they walk on water. That's very good news for the professional embezzler.

Be aware that when considering honesty and dishonesty by looking at handwriting, we can never make a determination with only one trait match. One of the challenges with neatness can be in the subjective determination of where neatness becomes "quite" neat, then "very" neat, then starts to ring those alarm bells at the "overly" neat peg of the scale. Don't fire all your employees with neat handwriting or subject them to unfair scrutiny just because you now have neatness paranoia! Neat handwriting is something our society and business culture values. So it could just be that you do indeed have a very loyal, very neat employee. Review Chapter Four for more details on how to determine if a hand seems too neat or if it's perhaps a genuinely neat writer.

Dishonesty as Reflected in the 7's

Where else might you look for honesty? Look at the 7's for starters. 7's represent the Principles. That's one place honesty can break down. Here are four 7's for you. One of them is a talented liar whom you probably don't want to trust as house sitter while you're out of town next month.

Perhaps it might help to know our panel? One is a politician and professor, one is a tree surgeon, one is a librarian and one is a women's fiction writer. Two women and two men here. PS: it's an honest politician. He's not the one.

Remember some of the cues you were given in other sections of the book. Remember which one would be very opinionated about principles. That needs a judgment tic. And a weak principled person often does not have a nice sharp 7. These are hints for you.

If you can't decide which feels the most dishonest, then turn it around. Which one feels the most honest to you? Work backwards.

Plays Well With Others As Seen in the 3's

While you're thinking about the 7's, let's look at another. Let's say you are hiring for a front office manager / receptionist and this person needs to be able to get along well with others, have a good outlook on life and be able to go above and beyond the call of duty. That's not too much to ask of a receptionist, is it?

So you have four more applicants here, totally different from the ones above. You pick up their files to check on their 3's because you've heard that 3's are about how we get along with neighbors and co-workers. Here are the four 3's you see. Who will you hire?

Let's say one way you've been told to know that someone gets along well with others is by having a "full rocker base" on the bottom of the three. That's true and it's a good clue. It should help eliminate some from consideration if you know what a rocker base is and what it should look like.

Let me tell you about your applicants here. Actually, there's only one of these in "real life" who would probably even consider applying for the front office job because all the rest are in very different professions. One is a church leader, one is a cabinet maker; one is a private investigator and one is a social worker. Again, two men and two women. While you think, let's get back to the 7's.

Answers:

7's: Did you guess which of your four applicants is dishonest? Left to right, the real professions are these:

- Female romance writer
- Male politician and business leader
- Male tree surgeon
- Female librarian and teacher

The dishonest one is the tree guy. Three things about that 7 are disturbing. It has that little hooked loop in the upper left corner; the top right corner is way too rounded and should be square; it could be confused with an upside down six. These are not good signs. Have him chop down your tree if you like, but I'd make sure that's all he's doing in the yard.

The romance writer is a powerhouse. Her 7 is tall and full and powerful, with a little tic in her upper left. But it's not a loop. The tic simply means that she's opinionated and will fight for her position. The upper right is still a good corner. Nothing dishonest from this powerful romance writer's 7.

The politician is one of the most honest guys I know. He's a superb speaker and teacher, forward thinker (notice the way the 7 slash leads to the right) and a very strong and principled businessman. (Good sharp corner on upper right of the 7).

The librarian, that fourth one, is quiet though she has a wild side she'd like to let loose (foot tic on the 7) and she can be quite a talker once she gets going. But you might have to see her 2's or 3's to know that. I've added those above. She has a very pleasant and playful 2, which leads forward into a very full 3. Notice that there's no big gap between the two. So this is a natural hand.

Now for our office manager / receptionist applicant. Which 3 would be the best applicant? First of all, did anything disturb you about any of these? I don't much like that first one. It's overstruck and way too dark. The last one is dark, also, but that's because it's firm, real and committed, with only that slight hesitation just at the top of the lower curve.

The true professions represented here, left to right:

- Male cabinet maker
- Male private investigator,
- Female social worker
- Female church leader

I would be concerned about the cabinet maker's ability to get along well with all kinds of people in a fast paced office setting because of the overstrike. This intense overstrike is disturbing. Why would he feel a need to overstrike it so much so firmly? It's not because he does it with all of his handwriting.

3333

I went back to pull all four of his 3's from the sample and found strangely that all of them were clumped thick. It feels like some intense temper and anger issues. For these four clumped overstruck 3's to show up in the part of the hand related to a work environment, this isn't the receptionist's energy we were looking to hire.

When I saw him recently and told him I was using this sample in the book I asked if he could explain why he clumped the 3's so. He said it was just where he was that day. Fair enough. So let's not judge him to always be that way. But still, if his application came in with that 3, we might definitely pass it up in favor of another.

The second one, the private investigator has a very light stroke (perhaps too light) and lacks a rocker base. The top part of the 3 is what of himself he'll put into the relationship. Notice that he's a very private person (tiny top curve) and is not apt to give much (base is thin and rockerless). The entire 3 is tentative.

The social worker is a talker with too much of herself in the mix (oversized top loop). She has a skewed rocker base on the bottom. Not horrid but not great. Probably not the best match.

The church leader, last, is definitely the best of the 3's. Hers is good and solid, nice and firm. The whole hand feels trustworthy

1234567890
1234567890
1234567890
1234567890

and dependable. All of her digits are shown above.   (I especially like the essence of those 8's. Powerful helper in crisis!)

Her 9 is interesting here, too. 9 is "Self and the World," as in professional role. Notice that the round part (world) of her 9 is way larger than the staff (self). This is clearly a selfless worker who has done her work and knows both the world and herself. Very nice hand overall.

Detail Person Under Pressure: An HR Lead

Let's say that you have one last opening in your business for a team lead in the HR (Human Resources) Department. This person must be able to deal with lots of details under pressure and get them all right while at the same time being pleasant and stable and, of course, trustworthy and honest. Here are your four applicants:

1 2 3 4 5 6 7 8 9 0

1 2 3 4 5 6 7 8 9 0

1 2 3 4 5 6 7 8 9 0

1 2 3 4 5 6 7 8 9 0

This is a hands down choice if you know what you're seeing. Let's take each point one by one.

We need a detail person. What will that look like? There should be a focus to the hand, consistency in slant, slope and size. No weird extras in the hand; details don't usually come with gilded handles. Let me show you one of those gilded handle types:

1 2 3 4 5 6 7 8 9 0

A gilded handle writer like this is not usually someone who will do well in tending details. She's too caught up in being creative, getting "cool" points. Details are best tended by someone with a strong and clear order about the hand. That should help to cut one or two of those above from the short list.

Next point was "needs to be pleasant and stable." Pleasant will usually be orderly and predictable like "details" but must also have a trait of being softer and without spurs or hooks or angular points. The gilded sample, for instance, has a few too many sharp edges to actually be considered "pleasantly able to get along." She's almost certainly high-strung and artistic, probably a good creative mind, but not the most calming force in the teapot.

Stable is easy to identify and describe. Again, orderly but it will also have a focused, flat baseline. No wandering. All the digits sit basically on the same horizontal plane. That should take care of things and eliminate all but one of the above four applicants. So let's see what you are left with.

By the way, our applicants here are all right handed people, (three men and one woman) and yet you'll notice that two of them tend to lean back to the left a little strongly. What's that about? It means this person is holding back, aloof, reserving a portion of their energy for something. Could be they reserve it for themselves, or could be that they have fears which keep them from moving fully forward. Or they could be holding back for a partner or an event they're working toward. Whatever the case: reserved. Their mind or primary focus is probably not at work.

We probably don't want to have someone reserving that much of their energy if they're to be a hands-on functional lead. It wouldn't necessarily knock them out of the running immediately but think about it: If a team lead continually holds back yet expects the team to pitch in, that doesn't set a very good example. It could affect morale and team cohesiveness. Accountants and the contract review team of an organization can be that reserved. But in a team lead position, we probably want a little more forward lean.

So, our four applicants again:

1 2 3 4 5 6 7 8 9 0
1 2 3 4 5 6 7 8 9 0
1 2 3 4 5 6 7 8 9 0
1 2 3 4 5 6 7 8 9 0

First let's deal with the need for "details." That will eliminate the top sample. Too many gaps to keep a good eye on details. Details would fall through those large spaces in the hand. This writer is now a news reporter, no doubt dealing with details. Maybe her hand has changed since this sample was taken. At the time, she was still a student headed toward journalism.

The next requirement says "needs to be pleasant." Not that these others can't be pleasant but by far the most pleasant is the third one down. It's even, warm, engaging and fairly stable. This is the handwriting of a male charge nurse, supervising several other hospice nurses.

Another requirement (other than honest and trustworthy) is that the candidate be stable. The two in the middle would probably be the most stable, although really none of these four would truly be considered totally "textbook stable" from the point of having a completely flat baseline. Certainly the top and bottom do not.

There are other tests for stability than just baseline. One of them is consistent and orderly vertical slope (slant) in the digits. The 1, 4, 7, 9 are a good place to look in a row of digits because they are all essentially vertical lines which should be parallel on the page (with an exception made for the further incline of the 7 stem).

The 1, 4, 7, 9 of the fourth applicant have mixed slant as well as having extra little stress foot tics on most. These will probably disqualify him because 1, 4, 7, 9 are special digits. They each have that prominent vertical stroke which represents the "self" in various life contexts. If the 1, 4, 7, 9 are just shaped uniquely or artistically altered somehow (like our gilded artist above) but still maintain relative slant, then this would not necessarily represent violations in terms of consistency and stability of self-expression.

1 2 3 4 5 6 7 8 9 0

1 2 3 4 5 6 7 8 9 0

1 2 3 4 5 6 7 8 9 0

1 2 3 4 5 6 7 8 9 0

In the bottom sample, there are too many little things going on with the 1, 4, 7, 9 to ignore. All four have the emotional stress foot. These are likely to indicate burdened self-esteem issues. Not always a good sign for a team lead or manager. But then, not a problem: this writer is not a manager. He's a research botanist and a very good one at that. He spends his time mostly in field work with lots of time to himself to ponder as he works. He deals with almost no people issues except a colleague here or there. Certainly he has no stress of leading a team. The managerial traits he does not have are not a problem for him in his job.

By this digit slant stability test, the hospice nurse (third one down) is the best choice. Though his baseline wanders, it's not a major wander. Just a little dip there in 8, sense of major trauma. But he's dealing with death all day every day. Need we wonder why he might have a little baseline dip around major life trauma?

Overall forward dexter slant and positive outlook seems very good. Compare his 1, 4, 7, 9 with the bottom one. A world of difference! This fellow handles issues in stride and doesn't mind some upsetting challenges along the way. The descender stem of his 9 is a bit short, but as before, that's a good thing. He has a way of abdicating sense of self in favor of sense of the world. Like we saw in the church leader's hand, this can be a very strong social leader trait when it is genuine. Since we're talking about HR here and not Sales, it's a perfect match. For a Sales Lead position we might want that stem to be much taller, stronger.

We haven't said much about the second sample. This is the handwriting of a sergeant in the Army. He's probably not your ideal HR guy. Not much warm fuzzy here. Two things about this hand which are worth noticing are his very strong 7 and 0. Good principles and good Big Picture view. Those are certainly good starter traits for a leader's strong success.

Beyond Hiring with Handwriting

How did you do with the hiring scenarios here? These few samples weren't meant to give you an exhaustive listing of all that you can find in handwriting. But they do show you some quick overviews of handwriting's usefulness in a work environment.

Try reaching out now to do some of your own research. Get some of those samples from colleagues and friends at work and see what you can learn together as you look at what traits each of you has in your hand.

Handwriting studies can be an enjoyable and interesting team-building exercise, too. Not only will you learn an interesting and useful business skill, but you will also be able to learn more about the richness and diversity of your team. As long as the exercise is conducted with respect for team members' privacy and integrity, it can be a tremendous success as a new vision for a team.

It can be a fascinating opening to learn about the skills, talents and communication styles of each of the individual contributors on a team. The vision can begin with an opening to share with one another a small *JAQS Sample* as a link to the *hand behind the word.*

11

Putting It All Together
Taking Your First Handwriting Samples

Handwriting analysis isn't best applied as a solo activity. It is possible to learn on your own. But if you have a handwriting class available to you at a local community college or open university, you may want to consider enrolling so that your adventures can be more rewarding and interesting as you pull together all of these pieces you have been learning.

Especially when class size is fairly small, participants have good one-to-one time to consider various questions, making sure everyone is on a similar track when learning something new. Observe one another doing analyses and readings, staying focused on the positive as much as possible, keeping in mind the feelings and needs of the writer.

A teacher or a mentor for your handwriting studies can be invaluable. Scientists, teachers, business leaders, artisans, shamans, dancers and handwriting analysts among others have for generations passed on their knowledge by working directly with a mentor or respected teacher whose guidance helped inspire and stimulate their learning. Certainly if you can find a mentor, there is no substitute for such a resource.

Look in the phone book under "Handwriting," ask around in

your community, check with your local library, or search around on the Internet. In some smaller communities it may be difficult to find a mentor but once you decide you want to learn more, ask around, put an ad in a local paper, put up a flyer in a local coffee shop. Sometimes you may discover a mentor who learned of handwriting in another country or decades ago who'd love to share their skills.

Creating Your Own Study Group

Even if you don't find a mentor or teacher you can still learn. Create your own study group with friends who may be interested. Check out or purchase every book you can find on handwriting. Create your own sample book and go out in your life and collect as many samples as you can. The samples themselves will often begin to teach you quite well if you use them to apply all of the things you are learning from this or another book on handwriting.

Studying with a group is useful because you can learn from each other. Share sample sets and stories with one another about your process and what you are learning in your studies. As a bond of trust and respect develops, you can dig deeper into handwriting details with one another. You can practice on each other, asking clarifying questions and experimenting with different learning styles. It is helpful to see the wide variation of how you will each interpret differently the subjective nature of the traits and samples you will be examining.

What one of you regards as a large middle zone, for instance, may seem to another as just ordinary. Or what one regards as normal spacing between the numbers may seem to someone else cramped or too wide. That's where it will come in handy to have someone to bounce ideas off of. You need those varying opinions and views in order to better calibrate your own sense of judgment.

Over time, your common reference materials will bring a common understanding of interpretations and terms. A group will generally be able to reach a consensus of what is "normal" or "large" or "extreme" more quickly than you could on your own. The more you study together, the easier it is to agree on terms and the more effective the group's learning becomes.

Get a Sample Book, Get Some Samples

So, plan to go on out now and get some samples. It is one of your first steps to embarking on an exciting new learning opportunity now that you've got an understanding of the basics. You've learned something about the mechanics and biology of handwriting. You've had the overview on values and ethics and seen some stories of handwriting in relationship and business. It's time to get down to what you came here to do: learn more about handwriting. The best way to do that is to start taking samples.

Before we can take a sample, we need to have a place to put it. Since the *JAQS Style* sample is the subject of this book, that is the format we'll use for taking samples. We'll need to have a little *JAQS* sample book. Appendix I at the back of the book tells you how to make one. Or if you prefer, you can purchase one from your bookseller or direct from the publisher.

Once you have a sample book ready, there is no better subject to start with than yourself. The people you will ask for a sample will often be glad that they are not the first one in the book and will appreciate seeing that you were willing to write there, too.

Your willingness to let them see your handwriting says to them that you believe in participating fully in your collection project. They may want to ask you questions about your handwriting to see if you will really tell them what "secrets" are hidden there in yours before they choose to let you take their sample or talk about theirs.

Sometimes before people give their own sample, they will want to flip through a book and look at other people's handwriting a while. As they do, they may ask you several questions about various other people's handwriting to see how you answer. They're testing you to see if they can trust you with their handwriting before they agree to do it.

Reminder of Ethics and Etiquette

Be aware of professional ethics. Read over the chapter here on ethics (Chapter Eight). It matters whether you start talking about identifiable samples you have in your sample book. If your potential writers hear you tell them some deep dark secret as you point to a named sample on the page, it doesn't take much of a leap of imagination for them to see you doing the exact same thing with someone else, talking about their own handwriting somewhere else. You may not get that sample.

And frankly, you may not get many more samples at all if you get careless about respecting people's privacy. Regardless of how tempting it may be to point at a page in your book and tell the people before you some juicy tidbit you gleaned from that page, you are highly advised not to do that. Your reputation as a confidant and reflector for people is only as good as you prove it to be by your exhibited behavior.

The only person whose handwriting you have full permission to say anything about is your own. So if you have some juicy dish you'd like to share with others about yourself as you point to your signature and hand, then feel free if they are interested. Otherwise, if someone else's name is on that page, then that one person is the only other person you should discuss those secrets with. Even with them, it is unlikely that you should always be telling everything you may see.

If another writer is looking through your book and sees a named sample and says something like "Whoa! What is going on with this handwriting!? It looks really freaky!" your response should be something akin to, "Yes, well, what do you think might be in there?" and try to give it back to them or keep it as a general comment rather than specifics about this particular person or their handwriting. People whom you ask to give you a sample will often want to test you.

Start a Sample Book With Your Own Sample

They will want to see your handwriting in the book and hear what you have to say about it to prove that you are willing to "stand naked before the world" as they feel you are asking them to do. And they will want to see other writers' samples in the book and hear what you have to say (or hopefully, don't have to say) about those before they write in your book for you.

So plan to set a good example by having your sample in the book and be willing to talk about it if they ask. You will also probably want to have some other people's handwriting in the book and be unwilling to talk much about those.

Another good reason for you to write in your own book is for you to get a feel for what it is like to give your sample. Just like you'll be telling other people: Try to be "normal" (whatever that means for you) as you write your first sample in the book.

The Value of Comedy in a Sample Book

For sample books which might find their way into sensitive settings, you may want to be aware of what you (and others) write. Even though as an analyst we typically don't read it, certainly there will be many other people seeing these books, such as all future writers in the same book. It may be useful to keep whatever is written in your books appropriate for a wide variety of readers.

I carry sample books with me all the time and I have some friends (like my friend Michael McMillan shown on the rear cover here) who write in my books every time I see them. I have many repeat samples of his in many different books. Like Michael, some people take me at my word when I say I don't care what you write and won't probably read it anyway. They often get silly or may shock people with some of the off the wall comments they write.

Even though I talk to a writer about the nature of what I see in their handwriting in my book, it can sometimes be days or weeks until I happen to read what some people write there. When I'm about to do someone else's sample and I hear a chuckle and a "what is *this* about?" as they're flipping through the book to find a place to write, I know they've come upon Mike's or one of my other sample book comedians' latest gems.

They do make for interesting sample books. You might as well encourage people to be as spontaneous as they can with their writings. A spontaneous writing from the present moment is always the best form of a true sample. And the secondary benefit is that it will serve to entice and entertain future writers, maybe even shock a few. And you can coyly say, *"Oh, my! I had no idea that was in there. A handwriting analyst never reads the samples, you know."*

I wove snippets of a couple of these writers into the body of the book. There are several more included in the cover. See what you can find. I did warn Andy, the cover designer, that some of the samples we have get a little graphic and he might want to be selective about which ones made the cover. I notice that there are a couple of the silly ones on the cover but you might have some trouble figuring out what all they say!

Some of my comedic regulars try to outdo one another. They love to flip through the samples and see who has been by more recently. Then they set out to up the stakes. That's fine. This is a very effective way to continue to acquire more samples. The more creative and spontaneous the samples, the more other writers are put to ease about what to write. They often decide it can't be too threatening a thing to do with such silly samples in there.

Choices of Writing Instruments for Samples

A note about what to write with: when you offer your book to someone for their sample, you want to try not to collect any samples in pencil, erasable ink, felt tip pen, or a porous wet pen that bleeds through the page (like Sharpies or permanent markers). These will often damage other samples in the book by rubbing off the page or bleeding through. You see some evidence of those here in some of the samples in this book.

If some people say they simply must use a felt tip because it is their chosen favorite pen, (and for some it is) then test their pen on your paper and see how many blank pages you will need to leave between samples in order not to bleed through and ruin nearby ones. Some paper won't bleed until several hours to several days *after* the sample is taken, so be sure to leave extra blank pages next to it anyway, just in case.

Ready for Beginning

When you have your sample booklet ready to begin taking samples, fill out that first sample page yourself. Then turn your attention to finding other samples from people you know. Start with those close to you, perhaps family or coworkers you see every day. Try to get people about whom you know a little something, so that you can compare what you know with what you'll see in the handwriting. Don't be concerned yet if you haven't a clue how to interpret the samples as you collect them. For now, just collect as many as you can and have them ready.

I will help start you off by giving you a sample of my writing here. I went to my scanned samples to yank an arbitrary one of mine and found this one from a few years ago. I took it the day of a special friend's death, after sitting death vigil there with him for the last few weeks. His sister was my main cohort as vigil sitting end-of-life guide. Her handwriting is here, too, on page 215. These two are a good example of our commitment to take new samples in quite literally all kinds of situations in life.

Can you tell from the sample that this day was a little stressful and emotional for me? My signature is very tiny and cramped, compared to the way I usually write it. Look at that wandering baseline. And the way the 4 at the bottom in the date seems to melt. My numbers above are all hovered together over at the left in the left margin, also and taper off to the right. This is a guy in grief.

1 2 3 4 5 6 7 8 9 0   [What's your favorite number?   Any idea why?]
1 2 3 4 5 6 7 8 9 0
1 2 3 4 5 6 7 8 9 0
1 2 3 4 5 6 7 8 9 0 ♦ Signature ♦ Printed Name ♦ Paragraph of your choice ♦ The Date

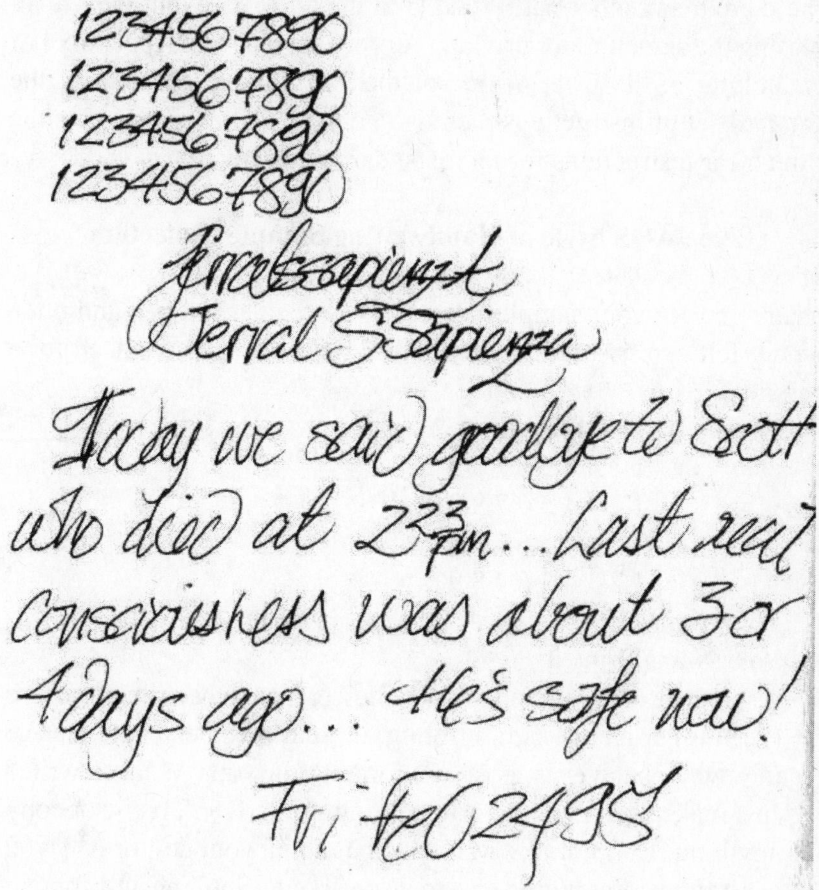

[Handwritten sample: numbers 1234567890 written four times, a signature, the name "Jerrald S. Sapienza," a handwritten paragraph, and a date.]

Today we said goodbye to Scott who died at 23:33pm... Last real consciousness was about 3 or 4 days ago... He's safe now!

Fri Feb 24 95

    I knew that this would be a date I would like to commemorate, so I took this sample just before dinner that evening. I tend to take samples any day I would like to commemorate and have a view of who I was that important day in my life. New jobs, birth of kids, death of friends and family. Even 9/11. I take *JAQS Style* samples on all of these special days.

The JAQS Sample Format

The sample on the left of mine is in the full *JAQS Style* format. There are many other partial *JAQS* in the book here, but they're all missing the signature for privacy. As you can see from Appendix I or by looking in the front of one of the *JAQS Sample Booklets,* the standard set of instructions there is to ensure that everyone gets the same clear instructions for their standardized sample:

The JAQS Style of Handwriting Sample Collection

Thank you for your sample. Please use a regular ink pen and not a pencil, felt pen, or erasable ink. Here are the 5 parts we need for a sample:

1) The ten digits (4 repetitions)

   1 2 3 4 5 6 7 8 9 0
   1 2 3 4 5 6 7 8 9 0
   1 2 3 4 5 6 7 8 9 0
   1 2 3 4 5 6 7 8 9 0

2) Your Signature
3) Your Name Printed
4) A sentence or paragraph of your choice. You may write in cursive (writing) or manuscript (printing) or your own personal blend of the two, whatever is most comfortable for you. What to write? Just make up something original right now. Don't recite or copy anything. Can't think? Maybe tell us about your day, or why you can't think of anything else to write about! Spelling and content is irrelevant. Just fill the rest of the page with something.
5) The Date.   And that's it!   –Thanks!

There is a reminder at the top of every sample page of the pre-formatted sample book to help writers remember the list of the pieces we need for the sample. You can point that out to them. Notice the little "Handedness L / R " note at the top right. It is sometimes useful to indicate handedness when taking a sample, especially when it leans way to the left and is right-handed or leans way to the right and is left-handed. It can also be useful to collect from every writer so that you have a consistent archive.

1234567890   Handedness: L / R
1234567890
1234567890
1234567890 ♦ Signature ♦ Printed Name ♦ Paragraph of your choice ♦ The Date

What You Need For the Sample

As for what to tell people when you ask for their sample: Tell them you're working on a new handwriting project and you'd like to have their sample if they'd be willing to give it. If you have chosen friends and family to start with then you already know something about these people, both how you get along and how you see their place in the world. So getting their sample shouldn't be difficult, especially if you are willing to give them yours for their sample books, too!

Most people want to learn more about themselves and are more than willing to participate in something like this. One of the reasons for starting with friends and family is that you already have a good basis for testing some of your early hypotheses about what certain handwriting means and looks like.

Go find your angriest friend and see if you can get some of that angry writing. Or your most flirtatious friend and see what a flirt's handwriting looks like. Or the most driven sales person you know, be sure and get that one. I can already see it. I'll bet it's oversized, leaning heavily to the right and not very readable. Those are the typical traits of the super-salesman personality.

Some people will ask you why you're using this tiny little format for their sample. Tell them a handwriting sample can be in any shape but you've learned that it's also useful to be able to have a common format across sample sets so that they can all be readily compared and contrasted. That's why you're choosing this format and are asking them to write in your *JAQS Style* sample book.

Your Sample Books as Valuable Treasures

When someone has agreed to write for you, think about what this means. It means that you are about to receive another priceless jewel for your collection of gems. The more samples you collect in this book, the more valuable the collection becomes.

Over the decades I have tried to collect samples from everyone in my life who has ever been important to me. I usually carry two or three sample books with me all the time so that I can take multiple samples if I'm out with several friends at the same time. I don't keep one book for family, another for co-workers, another for clients, another for people at church, etc. I mix all my samples into all my books. I have hundreds of books.

When you stir an entire life's people and personalities into books like this, as you might imagine, a sample book tends to take on a very personal flavor. When I go back and look at old books I can visit with people who are no longer in my life. Some have moved away or drifted apart. Others have died. But the jewel of who they are, who we were, still lives and grows more valuable all the time, there in the pages of my book. What a treasure.

It should come as no surprise, then, when I suggest that we should value our sample books tremendously. For instance, you may want to think twice about letting a writer run off with one of your sample books even if they agree to "get it back to you shortly."

If they mislay that book, you lose not only their sample but all the other samples in that book, too. Yet, when you ask some "busy" people for a sample they will ask you if you can leave your book with them and let them get it back to you. If you really trust them with your entire hard-earned sample collection, go ahead and walk away and come back later.

But I'll tell you, I prefer never to let my sample books get too far away from me. I like to get a sample immediately if it's going to happen, and take it with me. I figure if they don't have one or two minutes to write the sample now, there's not much point in leaving a book for them to again not have two minutes later.

I suggest moving on, but making a mental note to come back and get this sample another time. It could be an interesting one. It could be a Procrastinator, a self-important control seeker, a controlling Petty Tyrant, a Perfectionist, a Good Little Boy / Good Little Girl. But because of that initial behavior of putting off the sample, it's apt to be an instructive one.

Once You Have Taken the Sample

If there's anything you can tell this writer about their handwriting from what you've learned so far, great! After getting this far in the book you can probably recognize at least a thing or two. Perhaps something about one of the digits you've been concentrating on learning or margins, baseline, slant, size.

If not, at least let the writer know you're a beginner but you'd like to be able to get back to them later. As long as the samples are in ink and in a sample book or a binder, they'll keep. When you get together later with your newfound understanding, both of you can have a little "*Aha!*" moment as you make a comment or two to enlighten them about their handwriting.

Even if you don't know *why* you know certain things about a sample, try going with your intuition and then asking the friend who wrote the sample if your hunch rings true. Sometimes you can find you're on the right track and don't even know how you got there. Just trust that you are learning!

Trusting Your Intuition In Your Handwriting Studies

Getting the first feedback that you've been able to discern something about a writer's personality from their handwriting is a great feeling. It's an indication that you are paying attention and getting out of your own way. See if you can tune into whatever intuitive source you are drawing upon there and go back to the well. Come back for another sip or two while you're at it. It's possible that you may know more about handwriting than you think you do, once you get out of your own way and stop judging yourself as not yet knowing.

There will be aspects of just about any handwriting which will tend to stand out in some way. This is why we always seek to see what is the first thing which stands out about a hand. Without any judgments or expectations, we want to experience what it *feels like* (the *gestalt*). Cultivating this automatic reflex is very important to your successful study of handwriting.

Unfortunately, it's also one of the least trainable in a book. It is mostly a matter of faith, trust and commitment to your wisdom. You will find that the more you study handwriting, the more you will be able to "just see things."

But to be able to tell you how to get in touch with your intuition? That's a tough one to write. Try writing a description of how to recognize the taste of ginger or how to smell that it's about to rain, how to know you are in touch with God. Some things are just easier when we're able to rely on faith in our abilities, trust in our experience and commitment to continue to grow.

After cooking a time or two with ginger or watching and smelling an oncoming Midwestern thunderstorm or experiencing the bliss of mystical oneness with God, you don't need descriptions. You just welcome the next opportunity to be there again.

The most consistently useful way to acquire this kind of bliss with handwriting skills is to collect and study more samples, everywhere you go. Keep a sample book with you all the time, in your pack, your pocket, your purse, your glove box. Have it always on the ready to take out and catch that next new sample going by.

When Everybody's Hand Looks the Same

When doing your early samples, one thing you may notice is that the same trait keeps popping up in everyone's hand. This is normal though something you want to get beyond. Usually it means that you have learned one trait particularly well and yet are hesitant to grow beyond it to start finding others in a hand. You may find that you are always on the lookout for your favorite trait, sometimes whether it's there or not!

It might be time to step back and take that "first look" again. Clearly your interest in handwriting is intact. Now let's move beyond the first trait to the second and third and beyond. See the hand before you as the teeming dynamic story it is. Keep yourself open to learning even more. Pick another trait, study it well and let it be your new favorite for a while as you add to your repertoire. The more you learn about handwriting, the more and more traits you will begin to see in that first brief look.

Old Friends New Views

Perhaps the most precious gift of handwriting analysis is the way it expands our consciousness and our world to fit more of who we are. No matter how you saw writing and communication before, you see it differently after developing an understanding of the intricacies of handwriting. Once you know, you can never not know.

The first time you come upon an old journal, a note from a friend or a letter from a long-lost love, you will see it differently. The more pieces you fit into the puzzle, the more you see the bigger picture. Once the essence and feel of handwriting's story has seeped into your consciousness and vision, you will look upon your world with new eyes. You will see the pieces and they will all make sense as you put it all together and take in the beauty and the story of the *hand behind the word!*

12

Archetypes and Elements
Systems for Better Organization

C lassification and reference systems are always useful as we enter into any new field of study, in order to help build a shorthand system for ranking and filing. Using the system, we can then break down a larger job into smaller pieces for easier initial categorization and classification and make better sense of it. In handwriting, one of the useful shorthand for describing form and structure is the archetypal analogy of the four elements.

Used in ancient science and religion as a way of making sense of the entire world around them, the four elements helped people of that day understand and discuss behavior traits, emotions, actions and even natural events with a common intuitive vocabulary. The elements provided a context for discussion which, though often condescendingly labeled as anachronistic and archaic by science and religious leaders today, still provide a useful framework for viewing many aspects of human interaction, including handwriting.

Rating handwriting as fitting into or being influenced by a particular element is subjective, in that different readers will see different aspects and gradations of a trait and therefore may disagree. To make matters worse, it's rare that a hand would be considered to be entirely of any one of the four classifications, since most will be a blend of two or more. But still it's useful to consider which of the primary elements might be represented and what that might mean about a hand. Here are the archetypal four elements and some basic traits:

Element	How does it usually look in handwriting?
Air	Free flowing, often light, fragmented, slight
Earth	Squarish, heavy pressure, firm, often thick
Fire	Angular, sharp, often tall, hard right lean
Water	Round, puffy, bouncy, large, often vertical

You may have heard more about the four elements in another learning context. One popular systematized study where the four elements play a major role is astrology. There are three fire signs, three earth signs, three air signs and three water signs among the twelve signs of the zodiac. The elemental traits differ a bit in astrology from how they'll be used here, but if you are familiar with astrology, you may find parallels.

Some professional handwriting analysts prefer that astrology and handwriting never be mentioned in the same breath for fear of tarnishing handwriting's reputation. But I definitely disagree. I see no reason to shun or judge astrology any more than golf, cookery, auto mechanics or cosmetics. Astrology is a great way to help some folks learn some of the basic elements of handwriting.

Astrology has been around for centuries longer than any of our modern sciences. Its formal and organized hierarchy is infinitely more complex than most people understand. The progression of this big star-show in the sky and the mythological stories created to explain it have for many thousands of years captivated the imagination and devotion of elders and advisors, dreamers and youth, as far back as civilization itself.

Generations of scientists and religious leaders of the past, poets, politicians, kings and more than a few U.S. Presidents and other world leaders have kept astrological advisers close. Could it be that they would also have been interested in handwriting? I'd like to think that any inquiring mind would be willing to hear parallels and possibilities in any system which attempts to make sense of the complexities of human behavior and interaction.

So let's put it to use here as well. There are some common grounds. Astrology makes great use of the four elements in organizing its systems, so these will make a splendid background archetype for us to use in thinking about handwriting systems, too. Since the astrology signs already have personality traits attached which many people know something about, let's relate them to the four elements and then back to handwriting. Your understanding of both systems will prosper.

Let's go through each of the four elements, tell you which astrological signs go with that element, some of the known traits of each sign. Then we'll talk a bit about related handwriting and give you a sample of each. We'll start with Fire.

Bear in mind that these presentations here are not to suggest that all Geminis or Leos or Virgos will write like the one sample shown here. The samples here are merely representations in handwriting of some of the traits outlined in the personality listing of each of the signs of the zodiac.

So you could be a Scorpio and have a hand that looks more like what is shown here to be Aries. Or you could be a Taurus and have a hand that looks like a Pisces here. Take it all with a grain of salt and realize these are outlining general patterns. In a real astrological chart, you are much more than just your sun sign.

Perhaps in a future book we can go more into some of the other aspects of astrology like relating the rising sign, moon or Venus to specific parts of handwriting. That would be an interesting work. Rising sign, for instance, is the way people see us and so is our signature. Venus is related to our love life and methods. The number 4 and a "y" and "g" might bring out some of those things as well. But we'll save that for later. Now, on with the various elemental signs. We'll begin with Fire.

Fire signs: Aries, Leo, Sagittarius

Fire is a whole series of stories in itself. Think of the personality of the flash brush fire, the castle hearth fire, the fire of wisdom. Very different fires, very different energy among them. But that's also true of the fire signs of the zodiac.

Although all three are fire, they follow three very different patterns, from the brush fire which burns out of nowhere and takes over quickly like Aries; the castle hearth fire around which a dancing delight entices and entertains, like Leo; and the fire of learning and exploration which propels knowledge and discovery into the distant expanses like Sagittarius.

Common to all of the fire signs of the zodiac are the lapping flames which draw us in and yet push us away, cut us with searing heat if we get too close, yet warm us and inspire us too. What do you suppose that would look like in handwriting? We'd probably expect to see intensity and angularity, passion and an occasional uncontainable size. Probably some boundary crashing in the Aries and Sagittarius; maybe not so much in the Leo, although it tends to be oversized, self-impressed and always very visible.

Aries traits: Active, creative instigator, impulsive, intense, excitable, optimistic, can be aggressive, fiercely competitive, prone to tension and accidents. Selfish, driven to succeed. Can be driven by threats of violence, pain and danger.

An Aries hand: An Aries hand will often be oversized with a heavily rightward lean. It is likely to be hard to read because of its drive to make its point quickly but forgetting communication in the process. It is usually full of sharp edges and often has a middle zone with letters compressed right to left, a sign of motion, determination and drive.

The Aries hand is not about process but about product, so form is almost irrelevant to an Aries writer unless it happens to intersect with today's sometimes impetuous drive. The Aries writer will say, "What do you mean you can't read my writing? What are you, blind?" Then they'll tip over the jar of pens as they reach across the table to jerk the paper out of your hand to translate. Not known for tact or patience in the hand or speech. But they do get things done.

Leo traits: Creative, enthusiastic, contagiously entertaining, expressive, gregarious, extravagant, dogmatic and fixed in opinion, regal, proud, haughty, generous, self-indulgent, challenging and bombastic. Exuberant, inspiring, pleasure seeking and vain. Need we say intense?

A Leo hand: The most obvious trait of the Leo hand is its tendency to be oversized. If you have a signature in the sample, it is apt to be even more oversized, with the capitals of the signature sometimes exceeding 3x or even 5x the middle zone height, whereas a standard hand has a 1.5x - 2x MZ ratio. The Leo hand is also usually flowing and relatively readable, with an excess of flourishes, loops and tics, most often in capital letters and digits. Like so many Leo writers this sample is quite oversized, reduced here to fit.

Sagittarius traits: Energetic, adventurous, sometimes unintentionally bombastic and judgmental, hasty and impatient, opinionated and learned, pedantic. Lucky, optimistic, expansive, creative, philosophical, doesn't want to be tied down. Needs to move, speak, think clearly in order to be happy.

A Sagittarius hand: The Sagittarius hand will usually have a forward motion in it, with a firm belief that it has lots of material to cover, so may not slow down long enough to finish forming letters. The expansiveness often takes the form of exaggerated size, often with a pronounced forward lean. In this case, since we're looking at an Arabic hand, the forward lean is leftward. Baseline wanders a bit as he thinks and ponders. Normally a Sag is apt to wander up. This one varies.

Look at the far forward slant of the 10 (on the left here, the 1 and the circle or little dot, depending on which line) which represents world view. Full rounded 0's although they are a little flattened. It's a world view in motion.

In the second Sagittarius hand on the following page, it is interesting to note how small the digits are compared to the words. That suggests that she had a slow and self-conscious start. The digits also had a larger margin on the right, which suggests that as she started writing she warmed up a bit and felt less self-conscious. The good sharp corner on the upper right of the 7 suggests strong principles and opinions. That is borne out by the intense 8's and the opinionated and inquisitive (though a bit cynical) 2's. The 6's show some impatience the way the center loop is flattened.

This second Sag sample might actually seem a cross between Sag and Leo. Notice the over-size capitals with extra tics and loops in the capitals and digits (like Leo) and the talkative right-left compressed writing of the Sagittarius, always in a hurry to get there.

Fire Summary: Fire is a complicated and intense hand, altogether. It usually has an angular jagged edge and sharpness to it, often with exaggerated and showy strokes. Not usually very readable because of the compression and forcing together of angles and cutting lines. Size varies, but usually with high reaches, often with a tapering off in size, somewhat like lapping flames.

There is often an intelligence and an impatience and control in the hand. Fire handwriting usually feels hot to the touch. You can practically feel its intensity and if you rubbed up against it, it might cut, scratch or burn you with its sharp edges. Not always very pleasant or appealing unless you can handle the heat and intensity!

Earth signs: Taurus, Virgo, Capricorn

Taurus traits: patient, affectionate, stable, determined, practical, stubborn. Appreciative of beauty, can be jealous in relationship.

   A Taurus hand: Note the way this hand sits squarely in the middle zone (very little below base, little reaching up) and has a pleasant strong yet almost delicate presence. Like many Taurus hands, hers is also a fairly slow and intense hand. The "winged r" is a sign of affection as is the full rocker base on the 3 and the full loop on the 2.

   Notice also the way she started with a wider left margin on the digits, then moved comfortably over to start the note. The 8 and 6 are both signs of determination and even a bit of defiance possible in the 6. That, along with the tall stem on the 4 (relationship) translates to jealousy if she's crossed. Notice the frown in the foot of the 2, the downward stroke

1 2 3 4 5 6 7 8 9 0
1 2 3 4 5 6 7 8 9 0
1 2 3 4 5 6 7 8 9 0
1 2 3 4 5 6 7 8 9 0

Jevral,

I am sorry for the circumstances of our meeting,
but am very happy to have
met you + talked w/ you.

1.30.95

coming out of the 2. Although she likes to relate to and link with people (the loop bottom left of 2) she tends to be a little cynical about their follow through. (2 = impersonal view of people).

Virgo traits: reserved, modest, practical, discriminating, judgmental, industrious, analytical, want and need to know everything. Can be smothering or meddling if not moderated by other duties.

A Virgo hand: We again see the strong power in the Virgo hand, a full middle zone, a slant of relatively straight up. It's a slow, pensive, almost brooding hand, ever-analytical, meticulous and alert. The slow, big fullness of the hand is a sign of dependability and an ability to commit.

1 2 3 4 5 6 7 8 9 0
1 2 3 4 5 6 7 8 9 0
1 2 3 4 5 6 7 8 9 0
1 2 3 4 5 6 7 8 9 0

So Jerral, here we are again. Seems odd that we are reunited in the same location again. I look forward to settling down and makin' babies!

9-10-2002

Compare this hand (or any of the earth hands) to some of the air signs which have such a difficulty committing. No such difficulty here. In fact, getting a Virgo off-task enough to take a rest is more often the case. Tends to be very dependable.

Her baseline is wandering a bit, but form is good. This wasn't the most stable of days for her. But look at the sharpness of the 7 (strong, immovable commitment to a sense of principles) and the full ear-shape in the top of the 2 (loves to listen and hear people's stories). Together these suggest that she's probably apt to be ever willing to involve herself in other's lives. Delightfully nurturing at a minimum; meddling wouldn't be out of the question!

Capricorn traits: prudent, patient, strong in a cunning way, seeks honor, praise and approval, especially for security and reputation, is steady, dependable, opportunistic. Can be very good business people, especially when the money they risk is not their own. Their confidence is sometimes associated with how far up the social and business ladder they can climb. Their favorite way to maintain confidence and balance on that ladder is by having a large cache of resources they have been entrusted with by a wealthy friend or associate who leans on them to help out. But unless you knew that, you might think it all their skill, all their money. They usually know how to play the game and can go far.

A Capricorn hand: Capricorns in general would probably have made excellent scribes for the illuminated manuscripts of the Middle Ages, where presentation was a large part of their hand. They often have slow handwriting, which might be mistaken for being inauthentic since as we've seen before, inauthentic writers often write very slowly.

1, 2, 3, 4, 5, 6, 7, 8, 9, 0
1, 2 3 4 5 6 7 8 9 10
1 2 3 4 5 6 7 8 9 10

I have looked into what is called the soul. The experience is both refreshing and frightening. I recommend it to everyone.

April 11, 1991

But in the case of the Capricorn, it's just that they are very careful about revealing too much too quickly especially when it is only their own resources they have to play with. Give them the chance to invest your millions and you'll both prosper. Their handwriting will sometimes take on the flash and blossom of a successful business person: full, passionate, strong right lean, sometimes even in all CAPs. This writer here is more philosophical than business-pushy, though, so his richness is more intellectual and pensive.

He's also having some heart trouble: see the "o" in looked, soul, recommend? He did indeed have heart problems which encouraged him to retire early from his stressful legal profession and return to a more pensive life as researcher and teacher.

Earth Summary: Earth tends to be blocky, squarish, practical, even a bit heavy. May have heavier than normal pressure, but it's usually slower, even, considered. Slant is usually close to upright and spacing between characters is minimal.

Earth tends to have a kind of roundness like a water hand, but they are first strong, firm, pleasant qualities. Feel the relative stability and firmness of the earth hand. That is one of its traits.

Air Signs: Gemini, Libra and Aquarius

Gemini traits: lively and energetic, versatile, mind over heart, adaptable, a communicator, traveler, nervous, a self-expressive talker.

A Gemini hand: Notice it imposes its own kind of order and form, (versatile, imposing self-expression) can't be bothered to keep a consistent baseline (nervous, energetic) but it's generally upbeat in form. When you take a sample from one of these writers, if you feel the back of the page you will often be able to feel the pressure there. It's an energetic and passionate hand. Notice the way the middle zone is compressed (mind over heart) as evidenced by the way "e" and other vowels are flattened.

The top of the 2 is nicely ear-shaped and the bottom has a delicate loop in it. This says that although the writer has the indifference and distance in other places in the hand, he's still a communicator and quite well aware of how to relate to others. The charming "g" agrees. It's not a "normal g," but it has a lower loop to hook people and an upper swoop to flirt. Similar to the two structures in the 2.

Libra traits: Active, artistic, energetic but indecisive, easy going peacemaker, diplomatic, polished, charming, a bit fickle, faithless.

A Libra Hand: A very gentle and easy going hand with gentle smooth lines all through it. Nice smile in the 2, with the full "ear" shape so she listens well. But notice there's no loop at the bottom. She'll play but she's not going to commit since she prefers caution. This could also be interpreted as fickle and faithless. Lots of willingness to start, but limited energy to maintain the full demands of relationship. (Notice the way the 4 is tightly closed at the top). This says she's very picky about relationship and can be idealistic, fearing commitment when one comes along.

1 2 3 4 5 6 7 8 9 0

1 2 3 4 5 6 7 8 9 0

1 2 3 4 5 6 7 8 9 0

1 2 3 4 5 6 7 8 9 0

I believe this is the happiest time of my life!

3 JANUARY 1990

Still though, clearly a charming person to be around.

There is a pleasant airy openness of space between the words, a general feeling that the hand reaches up. The artistic "e" is charming yet cautious again, has that sharp tongue in there ready to lash out and vocally defend itself if necessary (polished, cautious, diplomatic).

Aquarius traits: Assertive, independent, progressive, original and creative, detached dreamer, lives in hopes and dreams, a humanitarian.

An Aquarius Hand: This hand is clearly assertive and visionary, a leader. Look at her 8's and 7's. She has the classic double snowball 8's which underscore her intensity and commitment to power. Her 7's are sharp, cold and simple, meaning she's capable of being very much in control of her feelings and principles. She's not going to get caught up in the world of feelings or emotions. Notice the way her "g" and "y" have a plain downward stroke with no frills or loops. Those, plus her 4 with its tall main stem and its shorter clean secondary stem tell the same story: Her view of relationship is that she sees herself as essentially alone in the world and knows how to take care of herself. Her hand is quite recognizable as standard, yet has an inventive and visionary flair to it as well.

1 2 3 4 5 6 7 8 9 0

1 2 3 4 5 6 7 8 9 0

1 2 3 4 5 6 7 8 9 0

1 2 3 4 5 6 7 8 9 0

Handwriting analysis can be very revealing

January 25, 1991

The combination of her creative yet very formal "a," the 6 with its flattened loop and her full round 0 say that she speaks meticulously and has a polished and strong vocabulary which she likes to use especially for taking a stance to defend the undefended.

The entire hand has a slight backward slant to it. Although she is left handed and that's part of it, her hand also signals a detachment and aloofness, reflected also by other characters in the hand like "H", "g", "y", 4, 7, 9.

So those are the **Air Signs**. Do you notice some of the commonalities in the three? All three of them are related in that they have no particular attachment to the rules of things; they tend to see themselves as above the fray of life, creators and mediators of the culture. They therefore may or may not follow what others have put out there as rules and boundaries. They like to talk their way around things, see other possibilities, create new paths, new strokes, new form.

Summary of the Air Hand: Tends to be free-flowing, original, often light pressure, most prominent movement tends to be in the upper zone. Usually lots of space in the hand with some very creative and unusual ways of perceiving space and shape.

Threaded formations (where the middle zone is flattened down into just a thread) or streamlined simplified strokes are common. To grow, they crave freedom, beauty, opportunity. They need to have space in the hand since they typically fear or loathe commitment and containment.

Water Signs: Cancer, Scorpio, Pisces

Cancer traits: Quiet, receptive, retreating, non-confrontational, kind, nurturing, emotional, very much a peacemaker. Fearful aversion to being judged for reputation, doesn't want anything to do with the reputation. All about nurturing and protecting the family and the home, not always considered very motivated. Can be moody and overly sensitive.

A Cancer hand: The Cancerian hand often is reserved and quiet, round, with very little ornamentation or ostentation to it.

It is usually a practical and playful hand as long as it is not challenged. If someone challenges the writer the size of their characters can recede to very tiny, very cautious characters and a leftward leaning slant.

Devoted mothers or pet owners often have a strong Cancerian nature to their hand. There's usually a feeling of being wrapped up in the hand, contained, taken care of, nurtured. It's usually easily readable and carefully enough written that the message always comes through.

1234567890
1234567890
1234567890
1234567890

Rubies are red, amethest are blue, I like big diamonds and gold is nice too.

3/24/91

Cancer wants to listen well, with an ear shape in the top of the 2. This writer has a nice rocker base on her 3's, suggesting she's a good worker and a friendly neighbor when engaged. The concentration of her letters is in the middle zone, which is the present, here and now, very much the domain of Cancer. Let the air signs and fire signs dream, plan and create. Water prefers to stick close to the "here and now" and feel its way forward gradually, with emotion as a guide.

Scorpio traits: Imaginative, pensive, passionate, emotional, subtle, persistent, intense, unfailingly deadly to enemies, stubborn, sexy, secretive, creative, jealous second to none (except maybe Taurus)!

A Scorpio hand: Often can have odd stinging loops and hooks and tics in the hand. Full, round, almost playful in a dangerous sort of way, creative about boundaries, can have some very strange ways of making characters, as if invented specifically for the occasion. Often intensely picky about 4's (sexuality and intimate relations), 7's (principles) and 8's, (major irritations, major traumas of life). Notice this writer has very sharp edges on her 4's and 7's, with a very strong opinionation tic on the top left of her 7.

1234567890
1234567890
1234567890
1234567890

I'm ok having hool on interesting day 66

8-3-95

Her double snowball 8's say she is always watching. Those snowball i-dots and sinister hooked "y's" say that she is very self-conscious in social relations, especially intimate relations, so it's not surprising her 4 is so closed, narrow and sharp.

She wants so much to relate to people, according to the full 2's and full rounded 3's, but she simply does not trust people, says the hooked loop in the upper left of the 2. That is a judgment tic saying that she judges people before she even meets them. The lower right little frown in her 2 says she has a rather cynical view that anyone understands her or will really be there for her. Most of her 3's say she's a hard worker and devoted friend. The last one is a little odd; it seems too slowly drawn.

Pisces traits: Imaginative, intuitive, emotional, receptive, adaptable, sensitive (sometimes to a fault), conflicting desires and goals, mystical, gullible, deep and spiritual, artistic (though they often don't know it).

   A Pisces hand: Usually very round, to a point where it looks as though if you were to drop it, it would bounce. This particular sample is a good example of a hand susceptible to guilt, like Pisces often are. Notice the bent cross-bar on the 4. That's a tendency

1 2 3 4 5 6 7 8 9 10
1 2 3 4 5 6 7 8 9 10

Ayer hablé con
estro. El está pen
en poner una e
y quiere que yo
ando. 23 10/ Oct / 92

to feel guilty in relationship even when she's not at fault. Willing always to take the blame to keep the peace, not unlike Cancer. Also like Cancer, the Pisces hand is usually very readable. Pisces is even more round than the Cancer hand, being the single most bubbly hand of the twelve. Pisces hands really like their loops wherever they can find them, although they are usually too cautious to create new loops like Scorpio. If it doesn't belong, then Pisces isn't going to risk the judgment of putting it in, much as the loops "look so pretty" to the Pisces eye.

   Even Pisces men who write in all CAPs will often have rounded edges on them because the angular seems harsh to the Pisces hand. They have a sense of beauty and order and artistry that allows them to appreciate placing writing on a page in aesthetically pleasing patterns, so they usually use margins and baselines quite religiously. That's one place Cancer and Pisces can differ. Cancer retreats into itself and sometimes forgets its margins or baseline. Pisces may cry all the way home, but she likes to arrange her tears in a pleasant looking row, just the same. That shows up in a hand as carefully placed forms on the page.

Water summary: The water hand is the one people generally can identify the most easily when they start studying handwriting. Water hands tend to be very emotional, round and flowing, a kind of a pool on the page.

It is usually large and quite readable, even when it gets a little too bubbly. It has that flavor of looking so buoyant and round that if you dropped it, it might bounce. When you take a look at the difference between fire and water in handwriting, the difference should be immediately obvious.

Astrology, archetypes and the four elements can offer a useful way to organize thoughts about handwriting for an open mind, since there are parallels in the various systems' ways of looking at patterns and personality. It's all a part of the whole of Wisdom, The Mystery, Life. These are another system's intricate pieces of the puzzle.

It's best that we don't try to take these astrological parallels too literally. These are not to say that every astrological sign has only one form of handwriting. Definitely not. It's just that the traits of the signs and the elements are useful symbols and parallels for seeing and thinking about traits and personalities in handwriting. The same concepts are reflected in many different systems.

However deep your understanding of astrology, archetypes and the elements, applying their ancient organizing system to a study of handwriting can offer new insight into the *hand behind the word.*

13

Trait Compendium and Glossary of Handwriting Traits and Their Meaning

Finally, as a quick overview guide, here is a trait compendium with definitions, common meanings and interpretations of traits seen in handwriting and the theoretical and validated meanings these traits will represent. A trait compendium can be a book or reference guide such as this one, or it can be an informal collection of mental notes and observations buried deep in the analyst's brain, or shared across a discussion group's years and miles and experience. For every hand an analyst looks at, there is behind it some reference somewhere to a personal or shared trait compendium by which the hand has been categorized and interpreted.

I offer you this trait compendium in a little more informal form than many books you will see. Its intent is to help discuss some brief points with you as though I were right there talking them over with you, hearing your feedback.

Some of the Traits To Be Watching

Let's look at some handwriting basics in some over-simplified explanations of what we look at in a sample and what some of the variations there mean. There are generally positive and negative sides of any trait, with some exceptions.

Slope (Horizontal Movement on the Baseline)

How we accomplish our goals; status of mental energy, stability of emotional foundation.

Slant (Vertical Movement and Lean)

Interpersonal communication tendencies. Manner in which we deal with emotional challenges.

Size of Writing In General

Writer's overall sense of self esteem as status in the world. What do they think of themselves and how they fit? Larger writing can be confident and stately or it can be pompous and self-impressed, depending on what traits accompany it.

Pressure on the Page

Intensity of personality. Pressure with good form can indicate vigor and vitality, determination and dedication. Pressure with questionable or lacking form can indicate panic, fear, alcoholism, or anger and control issues. Leaders and dictators can both have intense pressure. Their values determine which direction the pressure pushes, for the better or for the worse.

Height of Characters

Connection with higher ideals and spirit; method and tendency to strive for goals, aspirations, reputation. Artistic and shapely height generally means finery of ideals and artistry. Fragmented or particularly thin forms reaching high can mean detached and distractible thinking.

Width of Characters

Commitment to accomplishment and action and method of doing it. Stability, willingness to interact and participate. The middle zone of handwriting generally holds the greatest concentration of width in form, the trait being interpreted as stability and strength of action.

Practical and effective form represents strength and dependability. Misshapen, chipped or harsh form can mean brutishness and misappropriated power.

Stroke Link Meanings

Beginning strokes (in letters): Intention, mental focus, distractive traits which interfere with action. Tasteful and well-integrated shorter lead-in strokes show a willingness to belong and participate in a group or community. Excessively ornate or long lead-in strokes can indicate infantile dependency, conceit or attachment to mother (as in an excessive lead-in on a capital "M" for instance).

Lead-in strokes (in digits): are generally referred to as tics and tend to be an indication of intensity or judgment. In most cases, tics are considered negative or at least judgmental because of their tendency to prejudge experience and thought. In some cases, a tic can positively strengthen a commitment to a particular trait (as in the case of the 7, stronger commitment to principles).

Linking strokes: Communication technique and tendencies; method of getting along.

Terminal (end) strokes: Methods of execution / social principle, generosity (or not). Upward is usually more positive.

Spacing of Page, Line, Word, Character

Page spacing and placement (margins): Economy, respect for others, wallflower or not, social precociousness, tolerance & drive for acceptance.

Line spacing (between lines): Sense of connectedness in social situations; order, methods, direction in life.

Word spacing (between words): Relationship to family, friends, social situations, local environment.

Character spacing: Method of relating to the world. Introvert or Extrovert, etc.

Tri-Zonal Views of the Hand

The Upper Zone: Spiritual values, idealism, mental aptitude, theory and ideals.

Middle Zone: Daily life; the mundane; everyday values; basic activities.

Lower Zone: Inner and hidden drives, sexuality, materialism, method and nature of acquiring and holding onto things, friends, reputation.

A Conversational List of Basic Traits and Qualities

Angular: Angular handwriting usually has more of a sawtooth, sharp, pointed nature to it with a tendency to corner sharply and move abruptly on the page. Angular handwriting often means harsh, insensitive, selfish or domineering. (Compare garland, arcade, loop).

Arcade: A columnar formation of handwriting with a rounded top, as on an 'm' or 'n' or similar character and as a connecting stroke. Arcaded strokes typically mean hesitation, emotionality, fears, slow to learn, dependent. (Contrasts with garland).

CAPs: Capital letters are designed to be used within specific rules of capitalization. Except for those whose profession requires it, a writer who insists on using all CAPs for all writing generally either has control issues, is merely lazy, inelegant and boorish, or can be downright anti-social. Those who come from professions where CAPs are required yet who insist on using CAPs in all of their handwriting generally tend to be inflexible and/or overly self-identified with their profession.

Using CAPs for all correspondence is never a good thing. Some writers will use rounded CAPs, a modified somewhat softened version of CAPs, to try and appease and assuage their guilt for using CAPs in the first place. These writers generally have sensitive but driven personalities and can be workaholics nearly incapable of slowing down. They are usually at high risk for heart disease and stroke.

Cover Stroke: A cover stroke is a special kind of arcade stroke which reaches over the top of a series of letters, to form a sheltering cover, denoting a hiding writer with fears, self-consciousness and sometimes feelings of inadequacy, extreme emotional wound or dishonesty. Cover strokes are protective in nature and always make a statement about lack of trust.

Cursive: A flowing form of handwriting which links letters together as form in motion, in order to speed along writing intact with emotions, expressions and intentions more prevalent in the resulting flow. (Compare Printing).

A writer who writes exclusively and continually in formal cursive exactly as taught in fourth grade penmanship class is usually either a handwriting instructor, an embezzler, a very self-conscious writer, or perhaps all three!

Seriously, though, the hand generally considered most intelligent and expressive is neither all printing nor all cursive, but a personal blend of the two, with natural liaisons and transitions made between the two in context of a quick and intelligent hand. (See Personal Blend).

The excessively neat all-cursive hand is often referred to as the Good Little Boy / Good Little Girl hand. (See GLB/GLG). It is often the result of having received such extreme praise for having succeeded at the childhood transition from printing to cursive, that the writer took on a lifelong ambition for the perfection itself.

Felon's Claw: The felon's claw is an anger stroke commonly found in anti-social and incarcerated individuals. See page 80. It actually looks something like a claw or talon, usually formed by a sinister (left-arcing) hook in a y or g. It usually represents violence, brutality and identity confusion. Sometimes it points to sexual deviance when combined with certain other strokes.

Garland: The garland stroke is both a connector stroke between letters and a formation for making the 'm' and 'n.' Its meaning is usually associated with interpersonal communication and more outgoing effective relations. (Compare Arcade).

Good Little Boy / Good Little Girl hand (GLB/GLG): A hand that tries too hard to be perfect, usually written by people fearful of "getting out of the box" to take risks. Their greatest fear is being accused of having done something wrong. It is often a hand which lacks creativity since creativity often requires risks and "living life on the edge," a terror for the GLB/GLG. This is a hand whose commitment to conformity and "the way it's spoze to be" is everything, where reputation precedes action and long-held prejudice, cliques and habit reign supreme.

Be careful about judging just any neat writer to be a GLB/GLG, though. Some are just neat writers or handwriting teachers like this illustration. One way to test to know if a writer is a GLB/

1 2 3 4 5 6 7 8 9 0

This is a sample of

GLG or just a neat writer is to watch the speed. The GLB/GLG will usually be a slow struggling hand whereas this naturally neat writer's hand is both quick and natural for her.

Ligatures / Links: The connecting strokes, usually between letters in a word. The detail nature of the ligatures and links are often unique to a writer, therefore a good place to identify forgeries. General types of ligatures include arcade, garland, implied. Implied ligatures are shortcut partially or wholly missing links but which the eye and flow of the hand tends to imply as there.

Loopy: Excessively round handwriting, usually integrated with swirls, swoops. Usually relates to overly emotional and talkative persons.

Lower Zone (LZ): The section of handwriting which reaches below the baseline on which a small "a", "o", "e", etc. sit, such as an "y" or "g" or other letters with descenders extending below base. In handwriting analysis, the Lower Zone usually signifies the hidden desires of sensuality, sexuality. Symbollically, we can use the reminder phrase of "Sex and Persian Carpets" to help us remember what the LZ signifies. Compare with Middle and Upper Zones

Manuscript Writing: see Printing.

Middle Zone (MZ): The section of handwriting which forms the essential center part of a handwriting pattern, typically occupied by the small "a", "o", "e", etc. In handwriting analysis, the Middle Zone usually signifies everyday life and the basic method of being. "Here and Now" is the symbol for the MZ. Compare with Upper and Lower Zones.

Mixed Case Hand: A hand in which upper and lower case letters are distributed irrespective of normal capitalization rules. Though there are exceptions, it is generally considered to be a socially deviant hand because it ignores rules of normal writing and tends to crash boundaries. A fuller discussion of the Mixed Case Hand is available in Chapter Four, starting on page 73.

Personal Blend Hand: A kind of handwriting unique to the writer which is generally a blend of neither all printing nor all cursive, but a personal blend of the two with natural breaks made by natural strokes of this particular writer. The Personal Blend is generally a quick, creative and intelligent hand because it takes its cues of when to break and when to link not from a copy book rule but from life itself. Ever alert, ever willing to change, the Personal Blend hand may actually have totally different linking strokes or letter formations for different contexts in writing, showing signs both of creativity and adaptability. Be careful about judging a fragmented and inefficient hand to be merely a Personal Blend. The primary difference between fragmentation and Personal Blend is the speed and efficiency of the hand for overall effective communication. (Compare Cursive, Printing, Good Little Boy / Good Little Girl).

Printing (also known as Manuscript writing): Printing is handwriting which tends to follow the basic elementary typed form of lettering rather than the flowing or cursive form. (Compare Cursive) Writers who write exclusively in printing are often hesitant of their emotions and fearful of self-expression, since these are usually much more automatically included in cursive. The tendency to write in all printing is often the result of a childhood of being excessively pushed or judged to where the writer always had to succeed at all costs, with any miss or near miss considered only a failure. The organic root of the problem is generally a childhood trauma around the failure to transition neatly from printing to cursive, which occurs more often in males than females. The hand generally considered most intelligent and expressive is neither all printing nor all cursive, but is a personal blend of the two, with natural liaisons and transitions made between the two in context of a quick and intelligent hand. (See Personal Blend).

QDE Questioned Document Examining: A specialized field of forensics which involves the testing and identification of various printed material including handwriting. QDE identifies forgeries and other types of handwriting fraud, but also deals with paper substrates, chemical analysis, etc.

Sinister Strokes / Hooks: Sinister does not mean evil. It comes from the Latin, *sinister*, meaning "of the left" so a sinister hook or a sinister stroke in handwriting is one which has a leftward stroke to it, especially where that stroke typically would be a rightward or *dexter* stroke. Even though sinister strokes by definition are just leftward strokes, they also usually have quite negative, (shall we say *sinister?)* interpretations, related to such things as sexual impropriety, brutality or deception.

Size: Comparative measurements of the height of characters in handwriting. The average Middle Zone (MZ) height of any given hand is considered 1.0 with other measurements of the same hand made relative to MZ. Specific to the *JAQS Style*, measurements of digits compared to the MZ should yield somewhere between 1.7 to 2 x MZ. For instance, if a MZ character such as a small "o" is 5 mm in height, the digits height is usually between approximately 8 - 12 mm. Digit sizes considerably greater would be considered large; significantly less would be considered small relative to this hand's MZ. Signature sizes usually vary between

2.0 and 2.5 x MZ. Note that size of signature usually is exclusive of descenders; they are measured separately. Descenders in a general hand usually range from 1 - 1.5 x MZ; descenders of a signature range from 1.5 - 2 x MZ. General handwriting width measurements generally range 0.5 - 1.0 x MZ. (MZ is a height measurement). Comparison across hands requires assignment of a standard to use for MZ norm. Size will vary according to context, but general *JAQS Style* quarter sheet norm will generally have a MZ measurement of ~ 4 - 6 mm.

Slant: The vertical angular lean of a hand. Typical normative hand has a slant of approximately 15 - 25 degrees right of center.

Slope: The horizontal angular motion of a given hand. Baseline is ideally flat, i.e. a perpendicular 90 degrees from the side of the page, or a 0 degree angular slope from baseline. Ideally the baseline does not wander up or down much. If it has to do one or the other, then a slight up-slope is considered positive and optimistic and a down-slope is considered negative and pessimistic or mildly depressed. Significant downward slope especially of greater than a couple of degrees is usually indicative of emotional depression.

Spacing: Like other measurements in handwriting analysis, spacing units are typically measured relative to the Middle Zone height, or MZ. Average letter spacing is relative, based to some degree on the shape of the letter. For instance, a small "i" is apt to have different spacing than a small "q" or "z" because of their tails. But in general, letter spacing is usually approximately .25 - .50 x MZ.

Distances > .7 MZ would be considered excessive, with under .15 too close. These are only approximate guidance; you will get a feel for what seems appropriate or excessive relative to your norms.

Threadedness: A tendency to vertically compress the middle zone of writing to where it appears only as a thin unremarkable and indefinable line, with no apparent letters or words in it. The threaded signature usually appears for one of two reasons.

Most commonly it is because the handwriting is too fast and fragmented and hasn't taken the time to include real letters. But sometimes threadedness occurs when a writer specifically is avoiding telling the truth or disclosing a true identity.

This is a classic trait in politicians' hands when they are knowingly misrepresenting themselves or a particular political issue. Recall that the middle zone (MZ) of a hand is the place where the basic "here and now" of life occurs, so when the MZ is compressed out, that usually either means the writer is trying to cram too much amplitude into the given bandwidth of life and ends up with a net flatline, or the writer is specifically wanting to hide what is truly going on in the MZ of life and in so doing tries to self-censor, or could be just flat out lying.

Tics: Any one of several kinds of short, usually vertical, lead-in strokes on a character, typically at the upper left of a digit like a 2, 3 or 7. Also called judgment tics because they usually indicate a tendency to have prejudicial commentary or judgment without necessarily listening to the other side first.

Upper Zone (UZ): The section of handwriting which reaches above a small "a", "o", "e", etc. such as an "h" or "t" or any capital letter. In handwriting analysis, the Upper Zone usually signifies more the theoretical, spiritual, intellectual and belief systems. "Religion and Ideas" is a symbol for the UZ. Compare with Middle and Lower Zones.

A Closing Word

Now that you have begun the journey, perhaps you will agree that handwriting analysis can be a fascinating blend of story teller, psychologist, detective and personal advisor. It really does magically materialize out of a page to show us amazing new patterns we hadn't yet realized we were missing.

Handwriting fascinates us as the gift it offers between writer and reader. The shapes and spaces, form and feel of a hand embrace us with this very personal form of communication. I'm happy you have had an opportunity to share this joy and this journey with me. I suspect the world is better off for the experience.

Perhaps if you are comfortable in your greater awareness of handwriting analysis, you might consider starting or joining a discussion group at your local bookstore, high school, library, church or coffee shop. Like a foreign language, handwriting analysis is best remembered and built upon by committing to use it to learn and grow and share with others in order to reinforce the elements of what we learn.

It can be an enjoyable weekly or monthly meeting to get together to talk about the samples you're collecting and share with one another what you've learned. The more samples you collect and the more you are willing to talk about what you are discovering in the handwriting you see, the faster and better you will learn.

Where From Here?

People are already asking me when Book Two will be out so that they can see more samples and we can go into more of these topics in-depth. There is so much still unsaid about general handwriting traits and studies we've hardly touched on in this book. But there had to be choices made as to what all to include or this could have been a book much too long. Since the primary topic was the *JAQS* format, offering a good foundation there was the primary objective.

Certainly there will be more books on *JAQS* handwriting analysis. This is just an introduction. It helps to get conversations started and get your sample books underway. It offers a basis for beginners to get their feet wet and have some guidance in collecting samples without too much overwhelm. There will always be questions left unanswered. But they give you something else to ponder, to work with, to keep chipping away together as you learn.

There is a kind of an arbitrary magical number, a critical mass involved in the propagation of new ideas. You'll see evidence of that as you talk to more and more friends who also start studying handwriting. Sometimes it will take several different people asking you the same question several times before you begin to realize that you already know the answer. The more you look at handwriting, the more you'll realize you already know.

So, about that next book? We'll all know when it's time for the next book. Meanwhile, let's have fun with this one and tatter a few covers as sample books get passed around and filled up.

As more people collect and share their samples, their expertise, their new theories about handwriting, no doubt other books will follow. Some may be written by me. Some may be written by you or your friends, as you learn and grow and continue to share the gifts you have, the gift you are to the world.

Thanks for coming along on this adventure. Who knows where it will lead? If it does for you what it did for me, it will keep you always interested in taking *Just A Quick Sample* again and again. You'll peer curiously and spellbound into a *hand behind the word* as you learn more and more about *Handwriting Analysis JAQS Style*.

Appendix I

Creating a JAQS Sample Book

The *JAQS Sample* format uses a quarter-sheet format on white unlined paper. To have a place to take your samples, it's a good idea to start by creating or purchasing your own collection booklet. If you would like to make one, the basic materials necessary are these:

1) Three to five sheets of plain white paper
2) Colored cover stock (if you'd like a cover)
3) Scissors or a paper cutter
4) Stapler (preferably long-necked stapler)
5) Acetate or sheet protector (optional)

Fold the white paper into quarter sheets, folding it in half both directions: top-to-bottom first and then right-to-left. You'll have then a miniature page half as wide and half as tall as your original paper. Carefully cut these sheets then along the horizontal fold and you'll have two small sets you can place inside of each other, making a little booklet.

Repeat this for as many pages as you have and you'll have a little booklet with eight times as many sample pages as sheets you started with. For instance, one sheet becomes a booklet with four individual little pages, two sides, so you can take eight samples in this booklet; four sheets becomes a thirty-two page booklet, etc. You can staple the booklets together and put an acetate cover on if you like. The basic booklet is all you need to start learning.

On the front page, write out clear instructions so that people will know what they are supposed to do for a sample. The instructions from our standard sample booklet are those listed on page 239.

As the first sample in your book, it's probably a good idea that you write a sample of your own handwriting on the first sample page so that people can see an example of the kind of writing you need from them. This also allows you to "pick on" your own handwriting to help them see that you're not perfect. (You aren't, are you!?)

If you would prefer to use a ready-made booklet, those are available. A companion sample booklet for *The Hand Behind The Word* is listed on the order form on the last page. It's the *JAQS Handwriting Samples Collection Booklet*, ISBN 0971710767, LLX Press, $4.95.

Following this instruction page, there are five blank sample pages. You can either write some samples of your own or ask other people to write in your book so you can analyze their handwriting. Your sample on the first page is always a nice touch so that people don't have to come to an empty book.

The JAQS Style Handwriting Sample

Thank you for your sample. Please use a regular ink pen and not a pencil, felt pen, or erasable ink. Here are the 5 parts we need for a sample:

1)   The ten digits (4 repetitions)

  1 2 3 4 5 6 7 8 9 0
  1 2 3 4 5 6 7 8 9 0
  1 2 3 4 5 6 7 8 9 0
  1 2 3 4 5 6 7 8 9 0

2)   Your Signature

3)   Your Name <u>Printed</u>

4)   A few sentences or a paragraph of your choice. You may write in cursive (writing) or manuscript (printing) or your own personal blend of the two, whatever is most comfortable for you. What to write? Just make up something original right now. Don't recite or copy anything. Can't think? Maybe say something about your day, or why you can't think of anything else to write about! Spelling and content is irrelevant. Just fill the page with *something*.

5)   The Date.

            And that's it!

                              –Thanks!

1234567890
1234567890
1234567890
1234567890

Left or Right Handed?   L / R

Signature • Printed Name • Paragraph of Your Choice • The Date

1234567890
1234567890
1234567890
1234567890

Left or Right Handed?   L / R

Signature • Printed Name • Paragraph of Your Choice • The Date

1234567890
1234567890
1234567890
1234567890

Left or Right Handed?   L / R

Signature • Printed Name • Paragraph of Your Choice • The Date

1234567890
1234567890
1234567890
1234567890

Left or Right Handed?   L / R

Signature • Printed Name • Paragraph of Your Choice • The Date

1234567890   Left or Right Handed?   L / R
1234567890
1234567890
1234567890   Signature • Printed Name • Paragraph of Your Choice • The Date

Appendix II
JAQS Sample Archiving

Sample Archiving Guidelines

When you begin to collect handwriting samples, you may not yet know whether you plan to make this a lifelong passion. But just in case, you may wish to consider setting up an organizational system that will accommodate you growing your sample collection with an eye toward future reference.

The *JAQS Style* format was designed with archiving and reference in mind. Each *JAQS* sample booklet contains forty sample pages plus an instruction sheet so that your writers will each receive the same clear instructions for research standard sampling. As you begin new books, give the booklet a unique identifier label so that you can refer to and locate samples there more quickly. You may label it as a group name, venue location, date code or just an arbitrary name. When archiving, you can scan your samples and order them on CDs with the sample book's name for the folder name and the writer's page number, first name and initial as the filename. As in:

LincolnCityWC/01-SallyF.tif

The JAQS sample format is a very compact sample format and will allow you to store literally thousands of samples easily in a small space. You can literally keep two thousand samples in a shoe box. Fifty booklets with forty samples each = 2,000 samples. For labeling, you will want to include at least each sample's date and name. It is also useful to include the location or venue where the sample was taken if you can. That helps to keep a better perspective for years later when you may not remember why or where you took a particular sample. If you fill an entire booklet at one location or group, then let the book itself bear the group name. Or if you take only one or two samples at one place, then write a little note in the top margin of the sample with any pertinent notes such as

"SFO Writer's Conference" or "ATL Garden Club." You will thank yourself later for the notations.

As you continue to grow your sample collection, you will want to keep them in some kind of available order so that you can go back and look up particular samples relatively easily. You may want to do readings or reflection for repeat writers who come back to you for check readings. It is useful to be able to have the previous sample available so that you can immediately notice and address any significant changes in the hand. The changes will cue you in to what's going on in this person's life and what traits you may expect to see in other places in the hand.

You may also want to consider creating a database of all of your samples for comparative cross sample studies.

Whether or not handwriting analysis becomes your lifelong passion, a useful archive system is relatively easy to create. If you later turn your collections over to friends or heirs, they will be deeply indebted to your thoughtfulness and wisdom as you embarked on this lifelong learning fascination.

Have Fun and Happy Collecting!

Index

This page accidentally left blank.

:-)

Book Order Form

To order additional copies of this book or the JAQS Handwriting Samples collection book, take this to your bookseller or copy this page and send payment in US Dollars to:

L L X Press - Book Orders
Lifelong Learning Excellence, Inc.
Post Office Box 380
Eugene, OR 97440-0380

Questions? Tel: (541) 343-1202 / or email Orders@LLX.com

Item	Qty	Description	Price	Extension
HWA		**The Hand Behind the Word** *Handwriting Analysis JAQS Style* ISBN 0971710732 - 256 pgs	$16.95	
Sam48		**JAQS Handwriting Samples** *Blank Collection Book* ISBN 0971710767 - 48 pgs	$4.95	
		Subtotal:		
		$3 first bk; $2 ea add'l - Shipping:		
		Books plus shipping: Total Due:	US$	

SHIPPING AND HANDLING TO US ADDRESSES: $3 FIRST BOOK, $2 ADDITIONAL BOOK

Order Date:

Ship to:

_____

_____

_____

_____

In case we have questions about your order, please also provide contact info:

Tel: (   )   Email: _____

The **Hand** Behind
The **Word**
Handwriting Analysis
JAQS Style

v93.256